PRAIS

Kristine has reached into the secret place of God and found some unique insights on comparisons. Her gripping way with words will have you spellbound from the beginning and intrigued as to who she will pick next as her ideal character. You will find fragments of yourself in each one. Hopefully you will do as I did and ask the Lord to help you change the character flaws that you've created and accept the "you" He created and loves. Kristine has captured the true meaning of being an original and not a copy. This will be a book you will want to share with a friend.

PAM STOCKDALE, SPEAKER & CO-FOUNDER OF LATIN AMERICAN MINISTRIES

Comparing ourselves to others is an age-old problem. In Over It., Kristine Brown takes us on an eye-opening journey into the lives of three women in the Bible who struggled with their own feelings of inadequacy. As we get to know them through Kristine's delightful and often humorous storytelling, including stories from her own life, we can learn to appreciate each step of our own journey as God leads us in His way and in His time. Each chapter is full of practical application and Scripture to help us overcome our insecurities and embrace the unique person God made each of us to be.

SABRA PENLEY, WRITER AT SIMPLYONEINMARRIAGE.COM

Kristine has—as my grandmother used to say—"hit the nail on the head" concerning comparing ourselves to each other. She has made it a journey, she has made it fun, and she has made it encouraging. All of these things are needed to walk down a daily path of change. It's a needed change for each one of us. You see, in life, it's easy for us to miss our own uniqueness when we want to look in the mirror and see someone else. We miss our own God creation staring right back at us. We do not want to miss our own path that God has created just for us to walk. It's way too exciting to miss a moment.

LYNN MCKENZIE, CO-FOUNDER OF ROAD 2 GLORY
MINISTRIES & LM BARREL RACING

If you have struggled for the confidence to act when God calls, then Over It. Conquering Comparison to Live Out God's Plan is a must-read for you. Kristine Brown uses the lives of three women in the Bible to point out examples of what happens when we allow barriers resulting from self-doubt, that are created by our own comparisons, to guide our thoughts and actions. Not only does Kristine give real life examples of how this problem affects us in all aspects of our lives, but she gives specific, biblically referenced steps to overcome the struggle.

VICKI THRASHER, LIFE-LONG EDUCATOR, RETIRED SCHOOL
ADMINISTRATOR, MENTOR TO WOMEN AND TEENS

OVER IT.

CONQUERING COMPARISON
TO LIVE OUT GOD'S PLAN

Over It. Conquering Comparison to Live Out God's Plan

Cover Design by: Five J's Design
Interior Design by: Five J's Design
Editorial services by: Next Step Editing
Author Photo by: Kimathy Brody Photography

To Mom.

*For the love, support, encouragement,
and example, thank you.*

OVER IT.

CONQUERING COMPARISON
TO LIVE OUT GOD'S PLAN

Kristine Brown

TABLE OF CONTENTS

The Quest Begins Here

PART 1 – NOTICED MORE

Chapter 1: Stepping Out of Her Shadow

Chapter 2: My Kid Is an 'A'braham Honor Roll Student

Chapter 3: Contentment over Comparison

PART 2 – LOVED MORE

Chapter 4: Who Is *That*??

Chapter 5: Stay outta My Territory

Chapter 6: Cooperation over Comparison

PART 3 – BLESSED MORE

Chapter 7: All in Favor, Say *I*

Chapter 8: Remember Me?

Chapter 9: Commitment over Comparison

Chapter 10: What Waits Beyond the Quest

Notes

Journal

Heartfelt Thanks

About the Author

THE QUEST BEGINS HERE

"WHY DON'T YOU JUST GET A NOSE JOB?"

Her unexpected solution caught me by surprise. She didn't mean to hurt my feelings with her words. She responded according to what she knew, and beauty was her business.

To be fair, she *did* ask me what I liked least about my features. I sat in front of the lighted vanity mirrors with ten other teenage girls, learning the art of perfect makeup application. The mirrors themselves brought back fond memories of the many dance recitals from my past. Groups of girls in matching sequin dresses, anticipating the call to line up in the wings before gliding onto the stage.

Our moment in the spotlight.

Now at seventeen-years-old, her question coaxed hidden insecurities out and brought them to the surface. When I heard her speak, my eyes darted to the right and then to the left, glancing at the other faces in the mirror.

"What do you like least about yourself?"

It seemed like I studied their faces for hours, but in reality only a few seconds had passed. It took that short span of time for me to notice the intricacies of each girl's reflection and compare them to my own. Striking features stood out— blonde curly locks, dark olive skin, long eyelashes. Each girl had something special, but a strange thing happened with each noticeable characteristic.

The voice of comparison grew louder and louder.

Finally and without warning, everything I saw in the mirror fused into one condemning thought. The words blurted out before I could stop them.

"My nose," I whispered, hoping the others didn't hear me.

And with those two simple words, the comparison voice tucked itself deep in my heart where it would stay for years to come.

Looking back now, I wonder if the other girls in the class felt the same way. Did they also dread the embarrassment of pointing out our obvious flaws and attempting to cover them up? Or was I alone in the struggle with comparison?

This unwanted voice does not limit itself to tempting us into comparing our physical traits. Oh no, it doesn't stop there. Women feel a compulsion to compare ourselves to other women in every area of our lives—our relationships, our gifts and talents, our ministries, careers, families, opportunities, and accomplishments. Fortunately, as I grew into a young adult and desired a closer relationship with God, He began revealing this huge problem all women face. He also uncovered a deep truth the enemy does not want us to know.

We find the secret to conquering comparison through looking at the stories of women in Scripture.

Three of these women—though not in the spotlight— learned the key to erasing comparison and embracing God's plan for their lives. Their stories serve as much more than a lesson for us. They offer truth, hope, and the tools we need to make practical changes in our own lives. I will introduce them to you in the chapters of this book, and honestly I cannot wait for you to meet them.

Now before we begin, let me share a few suggestions to help you get the most out of the message you will find here. Each chapter is filled with layer upon layer of biblical examples mixed with lots of love and memorable moments. May I recommend grabbing a journal to keep handy as you read? I pray the Scriptures and stories will touch a place deep in your spirit and inspire you to learn more. Also, at the end of each chapter you will see Questions for Reflection, designed to help you absorb each lesson. Following each section, I've included related verses for added encouragement and prayer time. Don't have a journal or notebook available? Don't worry. I've got you covered. I do not want you to wait another minute before beginning, so no need to make that trip to the dollar store. I included several Journal Pages in the back just for you.

At this point, most authors would dive right in and tell you what motivated them to write their book. I believe this is important. However, the inspiration behind it cannot be contained here. It is found in each story woven through the pages of every chapter. Thoughts, situations, and wisdom told by women young and old grace the pages ahead. These stories connect us with one common, affirming thought: "Yes, I've been there too!" When this thought comes to you—whether in chapter one, chapter ten, or somewhere in between—my motivation for writing these words will become clear.

Right now, I want to invite you to come along with me on a quest. I call this a quest, not just a journey. A journey indicates going somewhere, and we certainly will. But in addition to what we discover along the way, we will also find something specific—something magnificent. Through this book and the stories of the remarkable women we meet, we will uncover the essence of comparison and learn how to say, "I'm over it," and mean it.

Over wondering why she got the promotion and I didn't.

Over wishing I had as many followers on social media as she does.

Over wanting my child to win the award this time.

Over waiting for someone to notice me.

Over it all.

As these three faithful women from the Bible illustrate all we need to know, I will translate their experiences into do-able steps we can implement today. I'm a practical girl, and I need easy action steps to follow. I hope you will find these useful, too.

Do any of these thoughts I've shared resonate with you? Have you felt yourself nodding in agreement? Then please allow me to tell you one more thing, with all the sincerity I can put into words.

I am right there with you, and I would love for you to give me the chance to share what I've learned. I offer a heartfelt assurance; you will not be disappointed. How can I make such a bold claim? Because every lesson learned in my life comes from a mistake, a vulnerable place, or a failure redeemed by God's grace. And the answers themselves come straight from God's Word, which "will not return void"

(Isaiah 55:11 NKJV). We are almost ready, but first let this Scripture give you a glimpse of our destination.

"But if you're content to be simply yourself, you will become more than yourself" (Luke 14:11 MSG).

This verse holds a big promise, bigger than anything our human minds can possibly imagine. So if you're ready, let's get started. Our quest is waiting.

And can I tell you just one more thing? I'm super-excited for you to turn the page…

PART 1

NOTICED MORE

CHAPTER 1

STEPPING OUT OF HER SHADOW

*"Keep me as the apple of your eye; hide me
in the shadow of your wings ..."*
PSALM 17:8 NIV

It was certainly understandable to feel less than her. At least, that's what I told myself. She was amazing, after all. Brilliant, funny, confident, the list goes on and on. As someone both respected as team leader and appreciated as a friend, our entire staff hated to see her take a leave of absence. A year without her fun personality and strong skills would be bad enough, but what happened next brought the agony to a whole new level.

"I'd like for you to consider taking over as team leader for a year in Susan's absence," my boss suggested with a smile. "Susan and I discussed this, and we both believe you can do the job."

Who, me? Team leader?

Although unsure of myself, I latched on to the confidence my boss had in me. This was my chance to find my place among accomplished women. My chance to do something memorable, and well, downright cool! I stepped into that role with the enthusiasm of a squirrel in autumn. *I could do this*, I reassured myself. Besides, I'd been working with Susan and the many other capable women on our campus for several years now. Yes, this was the moment I'd been waiting for. I embraced the opportunity I'd been given.

That lasted about a week.

Then, the comparison monster crept his way into my situation. Here are a few thoughts that invaded my mind:

You really should think about doing things the way Susan did them last year. Her way worked fine.

You might want to call Susan and see if she can help you with this.

Susan didn't have any problems because she didn't let people walk all over her.

When I heard these remarks in my mind, this is what I began saying to my heart:

You're not good enough because you're not like her.

I let myself sink deeper into the hopeless pit of comparison for a solid, mind-numbing year. When Susan came back to work, she graciously offered to allow me to stay in the leadership role. (Yes of course, she's kind-hearted and fair, too.) It took less than ten seconds for me to make that decision.

"The job is yours, Susan! Glad to have you back!"

Many of us have on-the-job stories like this one. My situation is not unique. Visiting with ladies from different places and varying backgrounds, I found out we all share a common thread of comparison experiences. The workplace is a major breeding ground for these stories because of the high level of competition we face at work. A friend and fellow blogger shared a similar experience. Because of a technological glitch at her job, others assumed she was not performing her new duties correctly. Though the mishap was not her fault, the comments she heard affected her in every area of her daily life.

> *More than once, I heard that I was not performing as well as the lady who did this job before me. I felt terrible and insecure, and I was harder on myself than anyone else even though I knew I was doing the best I could. We finally found out that it had nothing to do with me and I felt silly for being so hard on myself. I learned to focus on my job, ignore the criticism, and do my best. That is all I can control. When I compared my performance to others, it affected my whole day and I was less confident.*

Thankfully, my fellow blogger and I had something in common. We were both fortunate to have bosses willing to encourage and support us in our new-found roles. Some of us are not so fortunate.

In a survey conducted in preparation for this book, sixty-three percent of women surveyed said they had been compared to someone else by a boss, co-worker, or acquaintance. That startling statistic alone shows the amount of measuring that occurs between colleagues in the workplace. Sometimes those comparisons are real. Other times, as in my situation, innocent comments are misunderstood, giving the enemy opportunity to feed our insecurities. In either case, the only way to draw our attention away from those words and stay true to our God-given purpose is found in a constant, daily recommitment to Christ.

You were taught, with regard to your former way of life, to put off your old self, which is being corrupted by its deceitful desires; to be made new in the attitude of your minds; and to put on the new self, created to be like God in true righteousness and holiness. Therefore each of you must put off falsehood and speak truthfully to your neighbor, for we are all members of one body. In your anger do not sin: Do not let the sun go down while you are still angry, and do not give the devil a foothold (Ephesians 4:22-27 NIV).

In the above passage, the church at Ephesus received a lesson in daily renewal—replacing old ways with attitude and actions that reflect the love of Jesus.

But if I'm already a Christian, why do I keep falling into the same comparison trap? Why do I fight this same battle over and over?

If you've asked yourself these questions, you are not alone. Since the beginning of creation, when God brought man and woman into being, our desire to be valued and noticed has been a part of our makeup. God intends for us to find that value and worth through Him, but once other women made their way onto the scene, our flesh began to look elsewhere for validation. Women like Martha, Esther, Hannah, Leah, Rachel, and Ruth come to mind. And that's just the beginning. Although these women experienced the compulsion to compare, God worked in and through them, establishing an important place in history for each one.

Still feeling alone in this struggle with comparison? Then allow me to introduce you to a woman named Hagar. Hagar knew what it was like to walk in someone's shadow—

someone important, as a matter of fact. And living daily in someone's shadow can leave you feeling unnoticed and unneeded. We will learn a lot from Hagar's story. Not only about our common conflicts, but also about God's answer in our time of desperation. So let's strap on our sandals and travel back to around 1885 B.C., a time when Hagar found herself in a new role as servant and handmaid in the house of Abraham and his wife, Sarah. Our quest begins here.

SOPHISTICATED LADY

Because Hagar was described as an "Egyptian slave" in Genesis 16:10, we can assume she was acquired by Abraham during his time in Egypt. In order to get to know our new friend Hagar, we need to first become acquainted with Abraham, (first known as Abram.) Abraham had no formal title, but he would one day be known to all as "Father Abraham." God promised Abraham a big family that would one day become a big nation. He held onto this promise, and everywhere Abraham went people recognized God's blessings in his life. Abraham took his role as head-of-the-house seriously, as any honorable man would. When a famine hit the land of Canaan, Abraham made a detour down to Egypt. Egypt was a place of prosperity and would provide means for him to take care of his people.

"And sure enough, when Abram arrived in Egypt, everyone noticed Sarai's beauty. When the palace officials saw her, they sang her praises to Pharaoh, their king, and Sarai was taken into his palace. Then Pharaoh gave Abram many gifts because of her—sheep, goats, cattle, male and female donkeys, male and female servants, and camels" (Genesis 12:14-16).

This scene is an important starting point for us because it gives our girl Hagar an established background. Although Hagar is not mentioned in the passage by name, this is the only time Scripture indicates Abram traveling to Egypt. Hagar's time in the house of Abram most likely started here.

Egypt was an advanced society for that time, and Hagar was surely accustomed to a more sophisticated lifestyle than Abram and Sarai's nomadic tribe offered. If she served in any position in Pharaoh's court, then her ability level was up there with the best of the best. To say this was a demotion would be an accurate statement. According to Hebrew tradition, Hagar could have possibly been a princess![1] Can you imagine? If she were a princess, that would put her on even ground with Sarah, whose name meant "a princess." This name was given to Sarai by God as a sign of His divine purpose for her as the future mother of the nation of Israel.[2] Nevertheless, princess or simply a trusted servant, Hagar was in for a culture shock for sure. But I'm certain her fellow Hebrew slaves welcomed her with open arms as a foreigner, right? And her mistress Sarai made her working environment pleasant, right?

Whether our job is in the home or in the workplace, being the new kid in town is tough. I recall a story from a dear friend about a time when she accepted a position, excited for the possibilities ahead. Her new coworkers were not so excited. In fact, they showed their disapproval about having a newbie on the team. She felt left out, overlooked, and ignored. I can envision this is how Hagar felt also. And to make matters worse, her mistress Sarai put her in a difficult position.

"Now Sarai, Abram's wife, had not been able to bear children for him. But she had an Egyptian servant named Hagar. So Sarai said to Abram, 'The Lord has prevented me from having children. Go and sleep with my servant. Perhaps I can have children through her'" (Gen. 16:1-2).

Before we start bashing Sarai for this despicable decision, let's remember where we are. "In Near Eastern family law the practice (of offering the handmaid to the husband) was common and acceptable."[3] Though we may not understand the idea of giving another woman to your husband in order to have a child, this custom was considered common. With that thought in mind, let's get back to Hagar. This could mean a change in her circumstances! She's been left out by her peers and hasn't been appreciated for her skills. Could this be the break she's been waiting for? Becoming a second wife to the tribe's leader and future mother to his only heir?

THINGS COULDN'T POSSIBLY GET WORSE

Oh yes, we all know better than to utter these words, "Things couldn't possibly get worse." But they can, and for Hagar, they did.

"When she knew she was pregnant, she (Hagar) began to despise her mistress" (Gen. 16:4 NIV).

Scripture spares us the details of Hagar's actions. Did she flash condescending looks? Did she spew harsh words? Did she display a sarcastic tone? Her exact actions don't matter. What we need to remember is at this point, Hagar and Sarai are embedded in a deep comparison battle. We can't place blame or point fingers; we simply recognize the mutual suffering caused by this conflict between them.

Wait a minute. Where is God when all this is happening?

We are about to reach a pivotal moment in this account of two women who are more alike than they realize. But first we must notice that neither woman has turned to God for help or direction. The comparison monster came in undetected, and his voice has grown stronger and stronger in their lives.

Sound familiar? It does to me, too. It's times like these when we feel like giving up. And as we see in Hagar's story, she did just that.

"Then Sarai said to Abram, 'This is all your fault! I put my servant into your arms, but now that she's pregnant she treats me with contempt. The Lord will show who's wrong— you or me!' Abram replied, 'Look, she is your servant, so deal with her as you see fit.' Then Sarai treated Hagar so harshly that she finally ran away" (Gen. 16:5-6).

Pay particular attention to that last sentence. Oh, how the tables have turned! It was right for us to refrain from judging Hagar for her actions. We see here that Sarai too was involved in hurtful responses. Now, allow me to gently divert away from the little detail that Sarai blames Abram for this whole ordeal. That's a rabbit trail I'm not ready to chase! Let's keep our focus on the problem at hand. Hagar's had enough. *I don't deserve this kind of treatment,* she thought. She was over it. And so she fled to the desert, where God would make Himself known to her for the first time.

"The angel of the Lord found Hagar beside a spring of water in the wilderness, along the road to Shur. The angel said to her, 'Hagar, Sarai's servant, where have you come from, and where are you going?' 'I'm running away from my mistress, Sarai,' she replied. The angel of the Lord said to her, 'Return to your mistress, and submit to her authority'" (Gen. 16:7-9).

What?? Submit to her? The angel must've been kidding. There is no possible way a righteous and just God would send Hagar back to such an unfriendly work environment. Or would He? The angel addressed Hagar's questions with his next shocking statement.

"The angel added, 'I will increase your descendants so much that they will be too numerous to count'" (Gen. 16:10 NIV).

God had a plan, but Hagar needed to be willing to do her part.

One Day at a Time

Hagar knew what this meant. Day after day she would continue to endure ridicule by her fellow slaves. Month after month, she would face conflict with her mistress. Year after year, she would continue in the job she'd learned to despise. But now she had something that would keep her going. She had a promise from the Most High God—a promise of blessing and a future for her and her son. She would have to move past the hardship created by comparison with Sarai and do the job she'd been given.

"Trust in the Lord, and do good; Dwell in the land, and feed on His faithfulness" (Psalm 37:3 NIV).

Hagar did as the Lord commanded her. She returned to Sarai and Abram and gave birth to Ishmael. Her newfound trust in the Lord equipped her with what she needed to live a life brimming with purpose. Though she couldn't see the destination at the end of her path, she resolved to trust. And that kind of resolve in our faith walk can make history.

"Put your hope in the Lord. Travel steadily along his path. He will honor you by giving you the land ..." (Psalm 37:34).

Rely and Apply

In order to apply what we glean from Hagar's story to our own lives, let's commit the following faith statement to memory:

 Relying on God's promise is my first step in conquering comparison.

These few simple words sum up the theme of Hagar's encounter. But remember the admonition in Ephesians. This is not a one-time easy fix. We must commit daily to renew our minds against the voice of the enemy that tells us we are "less than" her. At the end of part one, you will find Scriptures to help establish this new mindset in your own life, but for now, here's one of my favorites:

"Your eyes saw my substance, being yet unformed.
And in Your book they all were written,
The days fashioned for me,
When as yet there were none of them"
(Psalm 139:16 NKJV).

If you had any doubt about your worth, God answers that doubt right here with bold proclamation. We have *substance*. We are *noticed*. We are *needed*.

Our Stories

Each one of us has a comparison story to share. Maybe you question your abilities as a wife. Maybe you doubt your skills as a teacher. Maybe you underrate yourself as a mom. Chances are these negative thoughts began with looking at someone else—someone who appears to have it all together. Like Hagar, our change begins with internalizing the truth of the Scripture in Psalm 139. Take a moment to read that Scripture once again before moving on to the next paragraph. Take your time; I'll wait.

"And in Your book they all were written ..."

All of our days were written in God's book before we were born. That's worth a fist in the air and a shout of victory! God knew we would struggle, and He knew we would fall. He made a plan of escape instead of condemning our fate. And that plan of escape begins with taking the first step.

In the team leader saga I shared at the beginning of this chapter, I misjudged that first step. But in true God-fashion, I was about to get another chance. Let's pick up where we left the story—with Susan's return and my sigh of relief!

My next year on the job with Susan back as team leader was relatively stress-free. She was once again paving the way for our group, ready to make all the tough decisions. And everyone knew she was more capable than me, anyway. Yes, things were back in order. I began to wonder, though. Could I have been an effective team leader? I started questioning how I handled my year in that role. Had I allowed the voice of condemnation to shift my vision away from God's plan? Was I following His will for my life? As I prayed and spent time alone with my heavenly Father, the answer became clear. I had run to a place of safety—a place inside my bubble of comfort where I would no longer measure myself against another woman.

(I can almost hear you snickering.)

The only safe place is in the arms of the Holy One, who guides and directs our every step. Under the shadow of His wings is the one setting free from the risk of falling into that dangerous trap of comparison. And with that first decision behind us, we can look forward to new opportunities. Next steps usually come when we least expect them. After one short year back on the job, Susan was promoted to another position, leaving the team leader job open once more.

Guess who was asked to take the job?

I know what you're thinking. "Here we go again." But don't worry, I learned my lesson! I accepted the offer with prayerful consideration and newfound wisdom—a wisdom that came with bumps and bruises along the way. Then, with a little help from my girl Hagar, I learned to embrace the path ahead. I served in that position for several years. Working with these remarkable women every day was a blessing! We formed life-long friendships. We cultivated an atmosphere of respect and love. We just plain enjoyed working together. How could I have missed all this before? When I no longer listened to *you-know-who*, my spirit opened up to the beauty of the ladies around me. And what a joy they brought to my life! Instead of seeing myself as *less than*, I viewed each one of us as more than enough in the eyes of our Creator.

Our path is a gift from God, and we will discover later in this book even more about its importance. For now, you will be relieved to know that we've not finished our time with Hagar yet. We are just getting to know her, and this is only the first part of her journey. Hagar has more to learn, and so do we. The next thirteen years for Hagar would be a time of choosing to embrace the beauty around her and appreciate her time as Ishmael's momma. But pretty soon, she would realize the danger of thinking her mothering doesn't measure up.

Have you ever wondered why another child is the top reader in the class while yours struggles with reading simple passages below his grade level? Have you felt the pang of inadequacy watching another child race past the finish line while yours lags along in last place? Do you ever heap the burden of responsibility back on yourself as a mom? Then come along with me, my friend. This next chapter is for us. Let's see what lies ahead for Hagar when another child makes his treasured entrance into the world.

CHAPTER ONE QUESTIONS FOR REFLECTION

At the end of each chapter of this book, you will find questions for quick reflection about what we discovered in that chapter. You can use these questions to guide you in your prayer time, or simply allow them to refresh your memory on the key point before moving on to the next chapter. Journal pages for taking notes and recording your answers can be found at the end of the book. Reflection questions for chapter one are listed below:

1. CAN YOU RECALL A TIME WHEN YOU COMPARED YOUR ABILITIES TO SOMEONE ELSE'S? Think back to that experience. What personal traits did you feel were less than adequate compared to hers?

2. FROM THIS LESSON, WHAT DID YOU LEARN ABOUT HOW GOD SEES YOU? Think of five words to describe how God sees you. Write them down. Remember them.

3. PROVERBS **23:18** SAYS, "THERE IS SURELY A FUTURE HOPE FOR YOU, AND YOUR HOPE WILL NOT BE CUT OFF." What does this Scripture tell you about God's plan for your future?

4. WHERE WAS HAGAR WHEN THE ANGEL FOUND HER? What did she do after the angel spoke to her?

5. HOW DOES CHANGING THE WAY WE VIEW OTHER WOMEN STRENGTHEN OUR RELATIONSHIP WITH GOD? Think again about the woman you've compared yourself to. In your mind or on paper, list five positive qualities this woman possesses.

6. OUR KEY POINT FROM THIS CHAPTER IS: RELYING ON GOD'S PROMISE IS MY FIRST STEP IN CONQUERING COMPARISON. What might that first step be in your own life?

CHAPTER 2

My Kid Is an 'A'braham Honor Roll Student

*"Instead of feeling like we don't measure up,
let's stretch the scale into eternity."*
ELIZABETH GIERTZ, MY MESSY DESK

IT WAS A CRISP SATURDAY MORNING AT THE SOCCER FIELDS. At five years old, this was my son's first season to play the game. We'd just recently moved to this friendly new town. I'd met many mothers with boys his age, and my family felt we'd found the right place for us to call home. When sign-ups for fall soccer arrived, I thought, *Why not? All the other moms are signing up their kids.* And so our adventure with organized activities began.

Our boy was always at least a head taller than everyone else his age. He looked a little out of place, and honestly was often mistaken for an older child. His towering frame was most evident in those traditional team pictures we bought every year. (Oh come on, you know you have a shelf full of them.) And even though he could have easily plowed through the field of kindergartners like a bull dozer, his gentle demeanor held him back. Aggression was not in his nature.

In this particular game, he happened upon the ball with little intention, but it was there just the same. Something welled up inside me like a volcano ready to explode. And then, it did.

23

"Go Garrett, go! Don't stop; don't stop! Take it to the goal! Come on, run! Go, go, go, go, go!!"

The eruption went on and on, until he kicked the ball straight into the goal on that pint-sized field. My husband caught the entire event on his cell phone camera. Not just the goal, but my embarrassing outburst, too. He had evidence to hold over this crazy momma's head for years to come.

Now don't get me wrong. I certainly believe we should applaud our children's efforts and cheer them on in their adventures. But I questioned my motives at that moment. What caused me to turn into out-of-control sports lady? You know, the one you want to walk right up to and say, "It's only a game, ma'am. And they're only five years old. Chill out." Why do we get so caught up in our children's accomplishments?

I'd like to say I figured out the answer to this question that day, and all other activities from then on were just hunky-dory. That wouldn't be the truth, though. It took many years of tough lessons learned for me to get my moments under control, and it all began with recognizing the root of the problem. Let's return to Hagar and her son Ishmael, now several years older, to see what else we can learn from her story.

There's a New Kid in Town

Genesis chapter 21 begins with the promised fulfillment of God's plan, not only for Abraham and Sarah, but for us as well. Sarah gave birth to a baby boy in her old age, just as foretold. Abraham named the boy Isaac, and the building of a great nation began. There was one, little issue. Ishmael—Hagar's child—was the firstborn son of Abraham. And don't think for one minute Sarah had forgotten about that. According to historians, Ishmael was approximately fourteen years old when Isaac was weaned.[4] Children at that time were weaned between three and five years old. Therefore, we can conclude he was around ten when Isaac was born.

"And Sarah declared, 'God has brought me laughter. All who hear about this will laugh with me. Who would have said to Abraham that Sarah would nurse a baby? Yet I have given Abraham a son in his old age!'" (Gen. 21:6-7).

No doubt Sarah beamed with joy at this blessing. Who wouldn't? I remember the first time I held my baby in my arms. There are no words to describe the feeling. It's a special kind of love—a kind that says, "I'll protect you, no matter what." Hagar had felt that too, but we can only imagine how she responded on Sarah's happy day. Did she join in the rejoicing? Were congratulations offered? We don't know for sure. But judging from previous experience, I'll assume Hagar had some trouble fighting off that voice of comparison. Oh yes, she'd heard it before, but this time it was personal. This time, it was about Ishmael.

Allow me to pause here for a minute to say that women are good at a lot of things. We are multi-tasking masters and list-making machines. We find a place for everything and keep everything in place. We make time to serve others, support our communities, and encourage our friends. We balance it all with grace and wisdom. But mess with our kids, and the CLAWS COME OUT!

PUT THOSE CLAWS AWAY, MOM

Kindergarten is a wondrous time—a time of discovery, adventures, and making new friends. Moms of kindergartners understand the rollercoaster of emotions that accompany sending your child off to begin his life of learning, and I was no exception. My boy found his niche in school-life. With the sweetest kindergarten teacher and a room full of potential friends, he was in kinder-heaven. Then one day, he came home with a problem. At least, it was a problem for *me*.

"Mom, a boy in my class hit me today."

"*What?* Was your teacher there? What did she say?"

"He got in trouble. He had to change his color from green to yellow."

"Well, that's it. You are *not* to play with him anymore. Do you understand?"

"But why not?" he questioned.

"Because he hurt you, and we don't play with kids who hurt us. I think it's best if you find someone else to play with. There are plenty of other kids in your class."

And the conversation was over, as quickly as it began. Do you ever let your emotions determine the next step in your plans without pausing and asking God first? Then you can relate to my response. But this is not how God wants us to react. Paul instructed the church on matters of worship in 1 Timothy chapter 2. We find practical advice in his words which will help us when our flesh wants to fight:

"I urge, then, first of all, that petitions, prayers, intercession and thanksgiving be made for all people" (1 Timothy 2:1 NIV).

Living a life of worship means bringing our prayers and petitions to Him first. Then by His grace, we will receive clear direction on how to respond. As the Holy Spirit gripped my heart, I knew my harsh reaction needed mending. I sought God in prayer and asked for help. He is so gracious to us in every situation, even our imperfect moments. God reminded me of my rash response, and when I took time to process the event I came to a revelation. It's kindergarten! These things happen on a daily basis. It certainly didn't trigger the end of the world, and those two boys were more than willing to forgive and forget the whole thing. With this grace-filled admonition from the Lord, I continued to pray. God was already at work putting His plan together, and I didn't even know it.

The phone rang. It was the little boy's mother calling. I'm not even kidding.

She didn't mention the incident, but she told me how much her son enjoyed playing with mine. He too was overwhelmed with all the excitement of kindergarten, and they were working together through the adjustment—like us. We talked for a long while. She suggested a play date. That sparked the beginning of a blessed relationship with one of the most remarkable women I've ever had the honor to call friend. And the boys? Now teenagers, they are still faithful pals. They are building a life-long friendship, and God gets all the glory. I learned a great lesson from that experience. Moms are not competitors on opposite ends of the playing field, but sometimes we let our protective instincts derail our decisions.

WINNER TAKES ALL?

Whether it's a child, grandchild, niece or nephew, nothing unleashes the caged animal like a threat to our kids. Women in Hagar's day were no different. And unfortunately, that's how these two moms saw one another—as a threat. They were both vying for the same person's attention and the same position within the clan. Not for themselves, but their sons.

"The child grew and was weaned, and on the day Isaac was weaned Abraham held a great feast. But Sarah saw that the son whom Hagar the Egyptian had borne to Abraham was mocking" (Gen. 21:8-9 NIV).

I find it interesting here that Scripture doesn't say Hagar was mocking, but Ishmael. Remember at this time, Ishmael is believed to be around fourteen years old. As a seventh and eighth grade teacher, I've spent several years of my life surrounded by teens, and I can tell you this: mocking is not abnormal behavior, especially when a younger sibling is involved! So on the surface, we may see Ishmael's teasing as the normal banter between two brothers, but there is a deeper point here we cannot miss. Isaac represented those born of the spirit. Ishmael represented those born of the flesh. Their sibling squabble mirrored our own future battle within ourselves. God knew our flesh, or sinful nature, would fight against our spirit. He gave us this familiar picture of two brothers to help us understand what we would face. Paul refers to this incident between the two boys in Galatians 4:29:

"But you are now being persecuted by those who want you to keep the law, just as Ishmael, the child born by human effort, persecuted Isaac, the child born by the power of the Spirit."

Being "born of the Spirit" means we are followers of God. As children born of the Spirit, we will be made fun of, just as Isaac was. Matthew Henry's commentary puts it this way. "The children of promise must expect to be mocked.

This is persecution, which those that will live godly must count upon."[5] Even so, Sarah and Hagar did not know this. They were two moms trying to give the best to their boys. The conflict arose, and the claws came out. Before pausing to count to ten, as I often have to do, Sarah blurted out a directive to Abraham that sealed Ishmael's fate.

"So she turned to Abraham and demanded, 'Get rid of that slave woman and her son. He is not going to share the inheritance with my son, Isaac. I won't have it!'" (Gen. 21:10).

I feel like I've heard this somewhere before.

Ishmael posed a threat to Sarah's younger, more innocent child. Without hesitation, she directed Abraham to send him and his mother away. Abraham showed his character as the head of the household by taking this matter to God first, prior to taking action. He'd learned that lesson before. Although he thought the punishment extreme, God reassured Abraham and gave him clear direction what to do. He was to obey Sarah.

"This upset Abraham very much because Ishmael was his son. But God told Abraham, 'Do not be upset over the boy and your servant. Do whatever Sarah tells you, for Isaac is the son through whom your descendants will be counted. But I will also make a nation of the descendants of Hagar's son because he is your son, too'" (Gen. 21:11-13).

We should not assume here that God's command in any way condones Sarah's behavior. God is God. Period. God moves in His way and in His time. Ishmael had to be separated from Isaac in order for God's divine plan to be fulfilled. The paths for these two boys were forged long before they were born. Abraham's role was to obey his Father, and he did.

The key point for us to take away is this: Take our prayers to God first, and trust His plan that follows. Notice God's gracious blessing as He reassured Abraham that He made provision for Ishmael, too, "But I will also make a nation of the descendants of Hagar's son because he is your son, too."

Abraham could go ahead and do what he needed to do. God had it all under control.

Now it may seem as though we've detoured away from our main character Hagar, but remember that she is sitting close by while all this transpires. For years she had walked in Sarah's shadow. Now Sarah's son seemed to be getting everything—more attention, more love, more blessing. Questions of comparison had every opportunity to surface.

Was Isaac more blessed than Ishmael?

Was Sarah more important than she was?

Were the other moms more noticed?

Were other boys more accepted?

As the slave, Hagar was subject to the wishes of her boss. As Ishmael's mom, she waited helplessly for Abraham to act. The next morning her fears were confirmed. Abraham gave the two some water and sent them off into the desert. I imagine in those extreme conditions it didn't take long for them to use up their modest water supply. Water meant life. The depleted life-source also depleted Hagar's hope for a future.

"When the water was gone, she put the boy in the shade of a bush. Then she went and sat down by herself about a hundred yards away. 'I don't want to watch the boy die,' she said, as she burst into tears" (Gen. 21:15-16).

Haven't we been here before? We certainly have. Hagar had forgotten one important detail—a steadfast promise. God had already promised Hagar that Ishmael would live to be a man. The last time she found herself alone in the desert, in fact. We discussed that in detail in chapter one. But when our current circumstances look bleak, we often forget God's past promises.

"For no matter how many promises God has made, they are 'Yes' in Christ. And so through him the 'Amen' is spoken by us to the glory of God" (2 Corinthians 1:20 NIV).

In desperate times, fear takes over. The crushing weight of hopelessness digs deep into our hearts. Our spirit wanes. Our strength weakens. The enemy's voice will worm its way into our thoughts, if we let it. I've been in the desert like Hagar, and I'm sure you have too. That's why the above Scripture is so powerful. By committing these words to memory and calling them out during our most despairing times, we silence that voice. It may have been years since her first visit from an angel, but God's promise to Hagar hadn't expired. God's promises never expire. We may feel weak and feeble, but God's assurance is strong and solid. The answer is *yes*, so we can shout, "Amen!"

LAND THE HELICOPTER

Walking through Hagar's second trip to the desert gives us a clear picture of the destructive pattern of comparison. Remember what we learned in chapter one. Taking our focus away from God and placing it on other women diverts our course. Here we once again see a woman who desperately desires to be noticed. Her son was overshadowed by a newcomer to the scene, and his entrance caused deeper self-doubt. We all want our children to be recognized for the special people they are, and this pure love for them can sometimes skew our judgment. Even those who walked closely with Jesus during his time of ministry here on earth were not immune to comparison's selfish ways. Salome, a faithful follower of Jesus, is a perfect example.

Salome was the mother of James and John, two of Jesus' disciples. What an honor! To have two sons walking so closely with the master? No man had reached a higher place of distinction. Two of the twelve. All I can say is, "Wow!" That would be like seeing your son standing atop the Olympic podium, a gold medal draped around his neck. Salome must've been completely satisfied with her sons' lives. No need for comparison here. If anything, other women most likely compared their sons to *hers*. But as we see from the account in Matthew chapter 20, Salome was also tempted by the desire for recognition. She almost fell into the trap of trying to earn greatness rather than trusting God's plan.

"Then the mother of James and John, the sons of Zebedee, came to Jesus with her sons. She knelt respectfully to ask a favor …'In your kingdom, please let my two sons sit in places of honor next to you, one on your right and the other on your left'" (Matthew 21:20-21).

In other words, Salome wanted her sons to have special treatment in heaven above the other ten disciples. Helicopter parenting may be a trendy catchphrase of our day, but it was prevalent even in biblical times. Salome meant no harm or disrespect to Jesus in any way. She simply wanted to step in and make sure her sons were appreciated. I've travelled that road a time or two myself. *O.K., more than a time or two. The kindergarten incident was the first of many.* But Jesus' gentle rebuke was just what Salome needed to remind her to trust in Him. And the conversation they had still applies to our lives today.

"But Jesus answered by saying to them, 'You don't know what you are asking! Are you able to drink from the bitter cup of suffering I am about to drink?' 'Oh yes,' they replied, 'we are able!' Jesus told them, 'You will indeed drink from my bitter cup. But I have no right to say who will sit on my right or my left'" (Matthew 21:22-23).

What an awesome reminder of God's sovereignty! Hovering over my child's situation will not help him grow into the person God designed. Our job is to guide. God alone determines the destiny.

Even though Salome displayed one minor lapse in judgment, she remained faithful to Jesus until the end. She was one of the few named women present at the crucifixion and the resurrection.[6] Her sons indeed fulfilled their destinies as determined by their heavenly Father and are remembered as heroes of the faith. Salome made the decision to land her helicopter and trust God.

Now let's return to the scene where we left Hagar, in a lonely state of defeat. Did she determine to trust God with Ishmael's fate? Did she put her hope in Him once more as Salome did?

A FINAL ASSURANCE

"God heard the boy crying, and the angel of God called to Hagar from heaven and said to her. 'What is the matter, Hagar? Do not be afraid; God has heard the boy crying as he lies there'" (Gen. 21:17 NIV).

It is interesting to note here the angel came because God heard *the boy* crying. Hagar was crying too, but the scriptural distinction serves to reassure Hagar of the Lord's concern for her son. Ishmael was her greatest responsibility, and she couldn't bear to watch him suffer. But God heard Ishmael and came to comfort them both.

Most mothers can recall a scary time watching helplessly as their child battled an unexpected illness or frightening prognosis. I remember a similar time several years ago. It was my first Mother's Day, and I didn't expect to spend it that way:

I sat in that hospital room watching my six-week old boy, laying there with IV needles protruding from both hands and both feet. Delirious from lack of sleep, I remembered the significance of the day. It was Mother's Day, and though there was no place I'd rather be than taking care of my most precious blessing, I slipped into a state of self-pity. My mind wandered to all the moms dining at the fanciest restaurants in town, laughing and relishing in the recognition. But there I sat, wondering why God would leave me here to face this challenge alone.

I imagine this is how Hagar must have felt. Day after day, serving and caring for Ishmael while the other moms seem to have God's hand of blessing and protection over them all the time. But not her, she thought. She trudged through the daily grind, facing one obstacle after another, never seeming to catch a break.

Were those other moms truly blessed more than she was? Was she left all alone by God to fend for herself and her son? No way, not our loving, omniscient God. He saw her.

Just as God saw Hagar that day at the lowest point of her life, He sees you and me. Let's look at verse 17 again, which serves as an important focal point for this chapter:

"God heard the boy crying, and the angel of God called to Hagar from heaven and said to her. 'What is the matter, Hagar? Do not be afraid; God has heard the boy crying as he lies there'" (Gen. 21:17 NIV).

We can rest assured as moms—God hears our children's cries. Whatever challenges they face in this life, He is their comforter and constant companion. He guides every step, and their futures are secure in Him alone. When doubt finds its way into our hearts, we have God's promise to hold on to. He fulfilled His promise to Hagar for Ishmael, and He will fulfill His promise to you, too.

"'Lift the boy up and take him by the hand, for I will make him into a great nation.' Then God opened her eyes and she saw a well of water. So she went and filled the skin with water and gave the boy a drink" (Gen. 21:18-19 NIV).

"Then God opened her eyes." Hallelujah! Hagar's hopeless situation had affected her sight. When He drew her attention back to His goodness, she saw what had been right there all along. God restored her life source. But the goodness didn't stop there. In verse 20, we see "God was with the boy as he grew up." He never left Ishmael, and He will never leave us. Yes and amen.

Mom Measuring—A Final Thought

Thinking back to that first soccer game, I realize how much I've learned since then. I confess that over the years I've battled with measuring my mothering skills. Not only that, but I've also measured my child. Like Salome, I once desired worldly recognition for him. Watching your child get passed over while other kids seem to receive praise is hard for any mom to swallow. Thankfully, I've come to learn from God's Word that my child's worth is found in Him.

"Rejoice in that day and leap for joy! For indeed your reward is great in heaven," (Luke 6:23a NKJV).

As Christ-followers, our home is not here on earth, but in heaven. For that reason, focusing on man's accolades only deters us from a grander reward that waits for us there. Let's teach our kids today that their worth is found in the One who created them—the One who gave them form, substance, and purpose. Our faith statement for chapter 2 is this:

 Focusing my gaze on God reveals my true worth.

We can also read it this way:

 Focusing my gaze on God reveals my child's true worth.

She may not read as well as her classmates. He may not run as fast as the rest of the team. That disability may cause delays in some areas of her life, but her value is far beyond anything we can see. And so is yours.

Now that we are keenly aware of the dangers comparison can cause, how do we move forward? What steps can we take to prevent comparison from distracting us? In chapter 3 we will explore practical steps to combat the type of comparison Hagar faced. First, let's take some time to reflect on what we learned from Hagar's life with the Questions for Reflection below.

CHAPTER 2 QUESTIONS FOR REFLECTION

1. CAN YOU RECALL A TIME WHEN YOU DESIRED ACKNOWLEDGMENT OR RECOGNITION FROM PEOPLE? Think back to that experience. How would you describe your feelings then?

2. FROM THIS LESSON, WHAT DID YOU LEARN ABOUT SEEKING EARTHLY RECOGNITION?

3. READ THE FOLLOWING SCRIPTURE PASSAGE:

   "Whoever wants to become great among you must be your servant, and whoever wants to be first must be your slave—just as the Son of Man did not come to be served, but to serve, and to give his life as a ransom for many." Matthew 20:26-28

   What do you think Jesus wanted His disciples to understand when He told them this?

4. THINK OF A SPECIAL CHILD IN YOUR LIFE—A SON, DAUGHTER, GRANDCHILD, NIECE OR NEPHEW. How would you react if he was being teased or picked on by another child? According to Abraham's actions when Sarah wanted to send Ishmael away, what are we to do *first* in these situations?

5. OUR FAITH STATEMENT FOR CHAPTER 2 IS: *FOCUSING MY GAZE ON GOD REVEALS MY TRUE WORTH.*

   Take a moment today to refocus your gaze on God. How will focusing on Him affect your daily life? If you are a mom, how will it affect your child's daily life?

CHAPTER 3

CONTENTMENT OVER COMPARISON

"Comparison is the thief of joy."
THEODORE ROOSEVELT

MY HOPE IS THAT WHILE READING THROUGH THE PREVIOUS chapters, you identified with Hagar on some level. Maybe you discovered an area of your life where comparison is holding you back from fully embracing what God has for you. Maybe you picked up this book because this whole comparison concept piqued your curiosity, and you are anxious to learn more.

Whatever prompted you to read this book, it will not be enough to simply study what God had in store for Hagar. Yes, that is a solid beginning. But to discover the depth of God's desire for our lives and see results in our spiritual growth, we need practical steps. In this chapter, we will learn the first steps to take in gaining victory over comparison. Let's begin with a review of the Faith Statements from chapters one and two:

 1. RELYING ON GOD'S PROMISE IS MY FIRST STEP IN CONQUERING COMPARISON.

 2. FOCUSING MY GAZE ON GOD REVEALS MY TRUE WORTH.

Both of these statements will be important to keep in mind as we look at three key lessons from Hagar's story. These moments were crucial turning points for Hagar, and they can also be applied to our lives today.

ISOLATION

Where was Hagar when the angel visited her? That's right—in the desert, *alone*. How many times have we prayed to God for an answer to a problem, only to fill our lives with so much noise that we can't hear Him speak? We are all guilty of this, and our busy schedules don't make it any easier. That's why step one is so critical. God often speaks in whispers. We must be silent to listen. And there is no way we can hear Him if we don't make time to be alone with Him daily.

Step One: Get alone with God.

When planning how to spend those much-needed minutes with God, don't allow yourself to fall back into the comparison trap! You will be vulnerable to feeling like your time isn't as long or productive as your friend's. Don't go there. Focus on you and what you can do in this season of your life.

If you are the mommy of an infant, toddler, or both, let me be honest with you. You may find it challenging to squeeze in some alone time with God. I'm praying for you now because I remember those days. You wake up to the sound of your baby calling to you from his crib, and another day begins. He's perched on your hip as you attempt to carry on with daily chores, all the time thinking, "Didn't I just clean this house yesterday?" When he finally falls asleep at night, you are so exhausted you can barely move to get into your own bed. Why fight it? You just crash on the couch, still in your pajamas from the night before.

I understand where you are. Unfortunately, I did not set aside time for God when my boy was small. I gave in to the pressures and anxiety of motherhood, letting that override my peace and joy. How different those years would have been if I had only relied on Him more.

Be encouraged today, mom. God sees you, and He is there with you. Your time with Him might be simply acknowledging His presence while you watch your baby napping, or uttering a sleepy thank you before giving in to those heavy eyelids at night. Whatever you choose, give the best you can. God is faithful to honor your efforts.

"And it is impossible to please God without faith. Anyone who wants to come to him must believe that God exists and that he rewards those who sincerely seek him" (Hebrews 11:6).

RUNNING TOWARD OR RUNNING AWAY

Although God met Hagar in the desert, we must make a distinction here regarding her story. Hagar was not running *to* God, she was running *away* from Sarah. In spite of this, God still showed His faithfulness and concern for her. Most of us are taught from a young age not to run from our problems. In fact, running away can cause even more issues.

Running away can delay reaching a solution.

Running away can inhibit our spiritual growth.

Running away can take us down the wrong path.

Make no mistake, Hagar acted on impulse when she ran away from Sarah. But her time in the desert provided the solitude to hear God speak, which is exactly what she needed. Her daily issues distracted her from God's voice. With all that stripped away, nothing came between Hagar and her God.

Getting alone with God acknowledges His importance in our lives. Even Jesus knew when to separate Himself from others to hear God speak. Luke chapter 6 describes a day when Jesus went to a mountainside to pray. In the middle of teaching and healing the sick, He once again faced the Pharisees who continued trying to trap Him with words. He knew just what to do.

"One day soon afterward Jesus went up on a mountain to pray, and he prayed to God all night" (Luke 6:12).

Those who do not have children at home may also run smack into difficulty when fitting time with the Lord into a busy schedule. Duties call to you constantly. Your desire to make a difference drives you to fill that calendar with more and more stuff. I can relate to this too, friend. Let's agree together today to make the drastic change we need and position ourselves to hear from God. In Priscilla Shirer's book *He Speaks to Me*, she shares the following statement:

"The one with the answer is right here, but the problem is that we won't sit still long enough for Him to give us what we need."[7]

How much quiet time can you set aside to be still in God's presence each day? Be realistic as you decide on an answer. Take a moment and jot down your thoughts. Look at your calendar. Try out this time for a couple of days. If it doesn't work, don't condemn yourself! Scratch it out, and try something else. Remember, God will help us when we take a step in His direction.

DESPERATION

Regardless of what got her there, Hagar knew just what to do once she came to the secluded desert land. She called out to God from somewhere deep inside. A place carved out by years of seeking the love and acceptance only God can give—a place of desperation.

Step two: Cry out to God for help.

So many times I find myself in a situation where I have absolutely no idea what to do. I'd like to say I'm one of those people who prays and hears God's audible voice giving me specific steps to take, but that's not always the case. I often pray for weeks, sometimes toiling over a decision instead of trusting Him to guide me.

In those desperate times when we scan the horizon, and the path in every direction looks bleak, only one thing will get us out of our mess. God's ways are more complex than our own. We may not be able to see a way out, but God has already set a plan into motion. All we need to do is call to Him. He will answer us in the most unexpected ways.

The great King David knew first hand of God's faithfulness and willingness to answer a desperate cry for help. In Psalm chapter 18, David tells of God's goodness in delivering him from the hands of Saul. Saul was David's predecessor as king. A deep-seated jealousy developed within Saul, and he pursued David relentlessly. I might as well tell you the ugly truth, no need to tiptoe around it. Saul hated David and wanted to kill him. There, I said it. I get shivers just typing the words. How terrifying that must have been for David, but God stayed with him! Even when David appeared to be cornered by Saul more than once, God came through and rescued him from certain death.

"In my distress I called to the Lord; I cried to my God for help. From his temple he heard my voice; my cry came before him, into his ears" (Psalm 18:6 NIV).

I imagine Hagar felt the same sort of hopelessness as she surveyed the land around her. Looking back, she knew she would face the same daily persecution from Sarah. Looking ahead, she saw only lifeless desert where no human could survive. With all she had left in her, she called on the one she'd heard spoken of so many times in her years as Sarah's slave. She learned then He was not only the God of Abraham and Sarah. He was her God too, and He cared for her.

As I write these next words, I proceed with delicate prayer. I understand you may feel cornered in a desperate situation in your life right now. Yours may go beyond what Hagar endured. You may see no safe direction, and feel that danger awaits you no matter which way you go. I pray God's wisdom and direction for your circumstances as you find those available with the resources and help you need. My heart aches for you today, but it also has hope. Hope that comes from knowing God has brought me out of a place of desperation, and He can do the same for you.

We cannot anticipate how God will work in our circumstances, but His Word confirms His desire for our best interest. Sometimes God works through others, sending the right person our way and giving them wisdom to help where we need it most. Other times He works through events, providing an opportunity where there seemed to be closed doors. Whatever His plans, we can trust they are good and perfect.

"For my thoughts are not your thoughts, neither are your ways my ways, declared the Lord. For as the heavens are higher than the earth, so are my ways higher than your ways and my thoughts than your thoughts" (Isaiah 55:8-9 ESV).

He is waiting for us to cry out to Him in desperation today. God wants to answer if we will trust Him.

REALIZATION

How hard it must have been for Hagar to return to Sarah and submit to her authority! As we discussed in chapter one, Hagar dreaded the thought of continuing in her role of slave to Sarah. How many days, months, or even years would she have to endure this torture? How could God let Hagar go through this?

Step 3: Realize God's plan.

Let's be honest with ourselves here. Sometimes our pride causes us to veer in a different direction because we think we deserve better opportunities. We don't believe God would actually ask us to stay in such a stifling place. Why, that would only hinder our ability to be used by God! I have difficult news to share. It's a lesson I've learned the hard way, and I'd like to pass the lesson along to you today. God sets the plan in motion, and our job is to accept it.

As one writer among thousands, it's so easy to see the way "everyone else is doing it" and decide to forge my own path. Countless how-to books have been written, offering the latest insight into becoming a successful writer. How to drive readers to your blog! How to become a published author! How to grow your platform! The list is endless and overwhelming.

Yes, these guides can be helpful. Yes, it's important to study your craft. But God creates the open doors that lead us to that unique place—the place where He needs us to be.

Believe it or not, we may not always be thrilled with following what God tells us to do. God is holy. Sometimes our human minds cannot rationalize how He works. God can see the end result. We can't. It's as simple as that. And because of this, we must daily release control of our lives to Him. He knows exactly what we are going to face when we follow His will, and He gives us everything we need to take that uncomfortable step.

Yes, I said uncomfortable. Thankfully, there is joy waiting beyond that step, and the next, and the next.

Sometimes one uncomfortable step leads to a lifetime of contentment.

So accepting God's plan raises a crucial question. How do we know when something is God's will?

Sometimes we get a feeling inside that stirs us into action. Determining if it is God's will or not is a huge challenge. Entire books have been written on the subject of understanding and following God's will. For our purpose here, allow me to share the main thing to remember when considering changing direction:

Does this action line up with God's Word?

God will never ask us to do something that is contrary to His Word or His character. Pray and let God reveal your heart. Determine your motives for making this change. Is pride causing you to want a different situation? A new job? A bigger home? Or do you sense the Holy Spirit nudging you to trust Him and take that step?

God is faithful. He will give us the answer and make the distinction clear. If we come to Him with a humble heart and an obedient attitude, we open ourselves up to accepting the plan God formed especially for us.

In her blog post titled, *Discontent, Dissatisfied, and Displeasure, Oh My!* my dear friend Ellen Chauvin puts it this way:

> Sometimes I struggle with being content. There are certain circumstances in my life that I don't particularly like. At this time, I can't change them. I'm held captive in the here and now. Struggling to free my tied hands. Chafing to do something that will bring about the change I feel I need. Frustrated. Discontent.
>
> One day I realized I was discontent with my discontentment. I was unhappy with my unhappiness. Something had to change. And it had to be me...

Comparison is one of three things Ellen lists that causes discontentment in our lives. She continues with these thoughts about comparison:

> All my friends have it! I want it too! Why can't I be like them? In writing, I've learned to call this yardsticking. Comparing my chapter one to her book series. Never mind that she's worked twice as long and hard as I have.
>
> Jesus Himself warns against this. Peter was concerned about what was happening with another disciple. Jesus tells him in John 21:22, "If I want him to remain until I come, what is that to you? You follow Me!" (NASB)

My job isn't to look around and see where everyone else is, my job is to follow Christ.

Moving Forward from Here

Concluding our study of Hagar, I would love to tell you I've completely conquered the myth that catapulted us into her story. You know the one. It goes something like this:

She is noticed more than I am. She is appreciated more than I am. God sees her more than He sees me.

As much as I'd like to say this thought is behind me, I still hear it from time to time. Overpowering comparison is a daily discipline. Even while I write this now, I am battling the comparison monster once again in my calling to write.

When I began researching this topic over a year before starting to write the book, I sensed in my spirit that God would teach me about comparison in a real, tangible way. I knew in order to share honestly about my struggles, I would face personal experiences that would test my ability to put these practical steps into action and trust God through the process. About six months before putting pen to paper on this project, I saw articles and blog posts written on this very subject. Not just any posts, but posts by well-known authors. Amazing women.

One thing you should know here. When authors contemplate writing a book on a topic, we will test the waters by creating conversations about it with our readers via blog posts and social media. So putting these clues together, I knew it could only mean one thing. Somewhere, someone with a recognizable name and published best-sellers was most likely writing a book on the same topic I was.

How's that for an opportunity to compare myself?

Here it is, folks. The moment when I pledge to put the

words into practice or unplug this computer forever. I believe with full conviction God is allowing this to happen in my life. I am actually experiencing what I describe while penning these words right now. God not only knew I would desire to help women strengthen their lives through overcoming the need to compare, but He also knew the exact date I would start writing this book. His words through the lessons we explore here give me the power to say *no* to comparison and *yes* to His plan.

If I go to the bookstore tomorrow and see a New York Times best-selling author's new book on the shelf with this theme, *I will still finish this book*. God purposed it, and I accept what He has planned.

One thing I pray you take away from part one is this: We are all plagued with this issue at some time in our lives. And as I mentioned in the introduction, Hagar was not the only woman in Scripture to contend with it! Comparison hasn't changed, and for that reason we can look to these great examples from history to learn how to attack it head-on. As we conclude part one, I anticipate the remarkable woman we will get to know in the next chapter. What important lessons we will learn from her story! Until then, let's end our study of Hagar and *Noticed More* with some inspiring verses straight from God's Word.

Below you will find ten Scriptures to read when you feel unnoticed. May these encourage you while you commit daily to embrace contentment over comparison in your own life. These Scriptures, combined with the three steps described above, will guide us through the rest of our journey.

TEN SCRIPTURES FOR WHEN YOU FEEL UNNOTICED:

1. "Your eyes saw my unformed body; *all the days ordained for me were written in your book before one of them came to be" (Psalm 139:16 NIV).*

2. "There is surely a future hope *for you, and your hope will not be cut off" (Proverbs 23:18 NIV).*

3. "But to all who believed him *and accepted him, he gave the right to become children of God" (John 1:12).*

4. "No longer do I call you *servants, for the servant does not know what his master is doing; but I have called you friends, for all that I have heard from my Father I have made known to you" (John 15:15 ESV).*

5. "Now you are no longer a *slave but God's own child.* And since you are his child, God has made you his heir" (Galatians 4:7).

6. "For he chose us in him *before the creation of the world to be holy and blameless in his sight" (Ephesians 1:4 NIV).*

7. "I sought the Lord, and He heard *me, And delivered me from all my fears" (Psalm 34:4 NKJV).*

8. "And this is the confidence that *we have toward him, that if we ask anything according to his will he hears us" (1 John 5:14 ESV).*

9. "But truly God has listened; he has *attended to the voice of my prayer" (Psalm 66:19 ESV).*

10. "But because of his great love *for us, God, who is rich in mercy, made us alive with Christ even when we were dead in transgressions—it is by grace you have been saved" (Ephesians 2:4-5 NIV).*

PART 2

LOVED
MORE

WHO IS THAT??

"Beauty is in the eye of the beholder."
MARGARET WOLFE HUNGERFORD

LET'S TALK FOR A MINUTE ABOUT THAT WOMAN AT WORK WHO always seems one step ahead of everyone else. You know the one, the boss's favorite. She gets chosen for every special assignment. She knows how to implement the new training and increase production with time to spare. It wouldn't bother me if she weren't so perky all the time. She may as well have a ray of sunshine beaming down on top of her head. She's just so *likeable*. Doesn't she ever have a bad day?

Maybe you haven't met her on the job, but she shows up for moms' group too. I'm sure you've seen her there—the one who arrives early and makes sure to help the group leader set everything in place. Of course, she had plenty of time to do her hair and makeup this morning, after clipping her kids' perfectly matched, hand-made bows onto their pigtails and packing their all-natural organic snacks into monogrammed backpacks. Meanwhile, my kid's bed-head bears a striking resemblance to some sort of rare peacock. How does she push a stroller in those shoes?

Maybe you've missed the last few moms' group meetings. You've still most likely seen her at school. She's everyone's favorite volunteer, after all. Bringing homemade cookies to the teachers and decorating for the school play. Don't forget heading up the fundraiser. Thanks to her, the school will get all new computers this year. Yes, thanks to her.

She seems to be everywhere. She's the most faithful prayer warrior at church who everyone turns to for her obvious wisdom and eloquent words. She always knows the best advice and the right thing to say. She's also the most talented writer, who strings words together in such a way even the most reluctant reader can't help but be drawn into her story. Oh yes, I know this person well.

Her name is Standard, and I've known her most of my life.

In high school she didn't just *sit* at the cool table, she *was* the cool table. Like most teenage girls, I wanted to be like Standard. In my opinion, she had it all. If she was tan, I baked myself in the sun, slathered in Johnson's baby oil. (Please don't try that today.) I doused my hair with Sun In spray to match her blonde locks. (You '80s girls know exactly what I'm talking about.) If she teased her bangs to a four-inch stance, mine followed. That's what teen girls do. We find where we want to fit, and we follow trends. Standard set the trend, and I followed.

But even with all her stunning physical attributes, there was something that made her even more attractive. Something coming from inside, but what was it? I soon realized my attempts at cloning her weren't working as I'd hoped. I decided it was time to show the world my *true self*. At least, who I thought my true self was at the time. Forget the blonde highlights. I donned one radical hairstyle after another. First it was clipping the back of my hair down to nearly nothing then shaving words into my hair. Next it was dying from one extreme color to the next. As if that wasn't enough, my clothing style changed from week to week. I wanted attention, and I couldn't figure out why Standard always seemed to get it.

As if our time together in high school wasn't enough, I decided to make her my constant companion. Does she sound familiar to you? I thought you might recognize her. Standard is not real, not in the physical sense anyway. She is an image we've created—a culmination of every pin, post, and picture we let saturate our minds. They blend together in perfect fashion, and the end result? An ideal we place ourselves next to so we can observe our obvious flaws. This standard may be different for each of us, but she's destructive in every way.

The next sister from Scripture we will meet carried Standard around with her as well. But through a time in her life when Standard seemed to be driving her every decision, something remarkable happened.

She's a woman dear to my heart, and I would love for you to meet her. Allow me to introduce Leah.

She Has That Spark

You may have heard her name before, but she certainly doesn't hold any fancy titles or prestigious awards for her place in history.

To meet Leah, let's fast-forward a bit from Hagar's story to 1928 B.C. Isaac, son of Abraham and Sarah, had grown to be an old man with two sons, Esau and Jacob. As our story begins, Jacob is about to venture out on an important journey to a place called Paddan Aram. On instruction from his father, Jacob determined to find a wife from the daughters of his uncle Laban. He knew from a recent holy encounter, God was directing him every step of the way.

When Jacob arrived at Paddan Aram, he entered into friendly conversation with some shepherds waiting to water their sheep at a well. He inquired about his uncle Laban. As if on cue, the men point out Laban's daughter Rachel who just happened to be approaching. It's obvious through Jacob's actions that he took an instant liking to Rachel. After all, he rolled a heavy stone away from the mouth of the well just so she could get water for her sheep.

"Jacob was still talking with them when Rachel arrived with her father's flock, for she was a shepherd. And because Rachel was his cousin—the daughter of Laban, his mother's brother—and because the sheep and goats belonged to his uncle Laban, Jacob went over to the well and moved the stone from its mouth and watered his uncle's flock" (Gen. 29:9-11).

Jacob acted out of kindness and respect to his new-found relative by rolling that heavy stone and watering the sheep. But we will soon learn about Rachel's undeniable beauty, so I can't help but wonder if there was more to Jacob's actions than just showing respect to his uncle. Could this have been a chivalrous deed as well? I can just imagine Jacob putting a little extra flex in those biceps as Rachel glanced his way. After Jacob's heartfelt introduction, Rachel ran to tell her father the exciting news of his arrival.

Jacob stayed and worked there with Laban. About a month passed, and Laban came to Jacob to discuss payment for all the time Jacob had been working for him. Laban also offered to let Jacob suggest an appropriate wage. This was Jacob's big chance to win the heart of the girl he'd fancied since the day he arrived. It also brings our main character Leah into the story.

"Now Laban had two daughters. The older daughter was named Leah, and the younger one was Rachel" (Gen. 29:16).

The next verse in our chapter gives us an initial glimpse of the relationship between Leah and her sister Rachel. The first reference to the two of them together describes how they are seen by others. Oh, what a stark contrast in these few words!

"There was no sparkle in Leah's eyes, but Rachel had a beautiful figure and a lovely face" (Gen. 29:17).

No sparkle in Leah's eyes.

Some biblical commentators believe the description of Leah indicates her lack of physical beauty. I disagree. None of the Bible translations say anything to indicate that Leah was not pretty. The King James Version uses the words "tender eyes" to describe Leah. The Jewish Midrash explains her tender eyes may have been due to "her weeping lest she be compelled to marry Esau."[8] Still other historians believe she may have been verging on blindness, as indicated by the words "weak eyes" found in the New International Version.

Amidst all the translations though, something keeps drawing me back to the description I shared above. Her eyes were void of sparkle. For some reason Leah turned inward. Her special qualities—those which would set her apart from all the rest—were concealed deep inside.

I picture Leah as that regular gal who just knew when she walked in a room with Rachel, all eyes would divert from her to her sister. The gal who tick-tocked through the monotonous details of each day, resolved to merely get by. The gal not seeing anything super-special about herself, her life, or her future. Not that she hated her life, oh no. It was nothing so drastic as that. It was just, well, regular.

But it's right smack in the middle of our regular that God likes to show up with some extraordinary.

TIMES TWO

In a few short weeks, Jacob had fallen in love with Rachel.

"Since Jacob was in love with Rachel, he told her father, 'I'll work for you for seven years if you'll give me Rachel, your younger daughter, as my wife'" (29:18).

Laban enthusiastically agreed. He knew the value of giving his daughter in marriage to someone of his own blood-line. However, after Jacob served Laban for seven years in exchange for Rachel's hand in marriage, Laban threw an unexpected twist in their well laid-out plans. On the wedding night, Laban sent Leah in to be with Jacob instead of Rachel. He tricked his nephew into marrying someone else.

"Now it came to pass in the evening, that he took Leah his daughter and brought her to Jacob; and he went in to her" (29:23 NKJV).

Here we have what I like to call a wrinkle. Like when your wrinkle-free sheets get that annoying crease right at the very top edge. So much for the wrinkle-free concept, right? I'm such a sucker for the promise of no ironing needed. I buy them every time. As much as I'd like to just crawl into bed and ignore the wrinkle, it's there. And it won't go away until I resolve to iron it out.

In Jacob's day, there were family customs to be followed. Laban explained to Jacob their family tradition to give the older daughter in marriage first.

You might have mentioned that a bit sooner, Laban.

He went on to offer Rachel as Jacob's second bride, but wanted another seven years of work in return. Jacob had a choice to make, but his love for Rachel made the choice easy. In fact, verse 30 tells us he "loved also Rachel more than Leah."

More than Leah.

Now Jacob had two wives—sisters, daughters of his Uncle Laban. One he loved. One he didn't. This signals the beginning of our look deep into Leah's spirit. We know who she was, and we know her situation. We know people talked about her sometimes like she wasn't even there. How did this affect her? How did she cope?

UNLOVED

Before we go any further into Leah's future with Jacob, I need to whisper a deep truth into your ear. I want you to get this, so lean in close. As we learned with Hagar, we don't often feel God is with us even though we know He is. It's one of those head versus heart things. We sometimes miss His presence because our focus is not in the right place. Just as God saw Hagar in her desperate state of comparison, God sees Leah too. Right from the beginning of her life as a married woman, we learn God saw her and cared about her situation.

"When the Lord saw that Leah was unloved, he enabled her to have children, but Rachel could not conceive" (29:31).

God is so good to us. Even when we don't see anything special within ourselves, He works miracles to show us how special we are to Him. He wants us to have joy in our everyday humdrum, and Leah was no exception. God gave her the ability to become a mom—something Rachel didn't have.

Yet at this time in her life, Leah was entering into a long-term competition with her sister over the affections of her husband. Her heart was not in the right place to see her ability to get pregnant for what it was—a gift from God. So Leah took this newfound gift as an opportunity to turn Jacob's attention toward her. She wanted to be loved, and she would do just about anything to make it happen.

"So Leah became pregnant and gave birth to a son. She named him Reuben, for she said, 'The Lord has noticed my misery, and now my husband will love me'" (29:32).

Leah's desire was clear. Her words indicate her need to win her husband's love, and she hoped this firstborn son would do the trick. She no doubt envisioned the adoration in Jacob's eyes as he first saw her holding Reuben in her arms—this bundle of joy who would carry on the family name. She acknowledged that God gave her the gift, but she used it to try to please her man.

MAY I HAVE YOUR ATTENTION, PLEASE?

Let's make a distinction here about a woman's role as a wife and her natural desire to please her husband. Pleasing our husbands is scriptural, and we should honor and respect them, putting forth every effort to show them love and affection. And yes, this includes doing nice things for them—just because. However, the motive behind our kind acts must be to follow God's plan for a strong, healthy relationship. My friend and fellow writer Jenny Shinsky shares this story:

When my husband and I were first married, he would compare me to his mom. He was used to his mom preparing certain meals a certain way and would always tell me her recipe. I know he was not trying to hurt my feelings and was only trying to help me. We talked about it and he understood. Now—after ten years—if I am making something I sometimes ask him how his mom would make it. Or I just call her.

My friend was not trying to win her husband's love through good cooking techniques. Rather, she chose to develop her cooking skills and her relationship with her mother-in-law. What better way to show kindness to our husbands? Her deeds overshadowed the comparison and moved them both to a place of mutual understanding.

I can relate to my friend's situation. Many of us have stories similar to hers. Early in my marriage, I knew very little about what it took to maintain a strong marriage. I'm sure most newlyweds feel the same way! I recall an occasion soon after our wedding when we went to visit my husband's brother and his wife. In my eyes, these two were superstars. Strong pastors, a loving marriage, two beautiful children, just an all-around amazing couple. I was stumbling through figuring out this whole marriage-thing. So when I walked into their kitchen and saw what my new sister-in-law was doing, I was mesmerized.

She was baking a homemade carrot cake.

Can you believe it? I didn't even know such a thing was possible! The only carrot cake I'd ever served was one from the bakery in the local grocery store, and those were only available around Easter. I was instantly drawn to her obvious wife-expertise.

The next day of our visit, my husband Phil and I decided to display our culinary skills and cook our siblings some Texas-style enchiladas. Of course, it was Phil's recipe. I was just the sidekick, or sous-chef if we want to get all fancy about it. Phil knew that to truly make the tortillas pliable, they needed to be coated in vegetable oil first. I had the idea to save a few calories, so I encouraged him to forego the oil coating and use the tortillas straight from the package.

Big mistake.

The enchiladas turned out dry and a bit crunchy around the edges. Not exactly a shining performance in the kitchen. Always the patient husband, Phil was never one to blame me. But his look of disappointment in the finished product sent me spiraling deep into a pit of self-doubt.

This was the first of many epic kitchen fails for me, but before long, a genuine desire to provide healthy meals for my family replaced my desire to emulate others in the kitchen. Now, twenty-two years later, every night my husband says the same thing when we finish our dinner, "This is my favorite meal of all the things you cook."

Then my teenage son quips back, "Dad, you say that every time!" And even after twenty plus years of marriage, it never gets old. By committing everything I do to God, I'm letting go of the desire to please others. This opens my heart to a natural love for giving and serving—for all the right reasons.

Remember what we learned from Hagar. Focusing our gaze on God reveals our true worth. If we determine our worth based on how our mates see us, we will live a life unfulfilled, striving for attention that may never come.

ANOTHER CHANCE

"She soon became pregnant again and gave birth to another son. She named him Simeon, for she said, 'The Lord heard that I was unloved and has given me another son'" (29:33).

Soon after Reuben was born, she became pregnant with her second child, another son. She named him Simeon. Leah's words once more proclaim her ongoing wishes to earn Jacob's love. With the birth of each new child, she hoped he would give her the attention she longed to have. When these hopes went unnoticed again, she became pregnant a third time.

"Then she became pregnant a third time and gave birth to another son. He was named Levi, for she said, 'Surely *this time* my husband will feel affection for me, since I have given him three sons!'" (29:34).

Notice the urgency in Leah's voice? With each passing pregnancy, she became more and more frustrated with Jacob's lack of attention. She'd had not one or two, but *three* sons. How much more would it take to win his affection? It's in these desperate times we need to make the crucial decision to cry out to God. And as we can see from Leah's next pregnancy, that's exactly what she did.

Leah realized she was letting her worth be determined by someone else other than God. After their third son was born, she finally became aware of the purpose of God's blessing— and it wasn't to get her husband to notice. Her change in perspective showed through her words when she welcomed her fourth baby, little Judah.

"Once again Leah became pregnant and gave birth to another son. She named him Judah, for she said, 'Now I will praise the Lord!' And then she stopped having children" (29:35).

We find our key lesson for this chapter in these few simple words uttered by Leah. "*Now, I will praise the Lord!*" As if to say, *OK God. This time, I get it.* Leah finally understood her actions would not win her husband over. It would not make her any more attractive than Rachel, either. What mattered most was her relationship with God, the One who would always love her no matter what. She emphasized her commitment to God by naming her son Judah, which means *praise*.[9] Leah chose to let go of her obsession with earning love from Jacob and purposed to praise her King. That decision made all the difference. Let's commit the faith statement below to memory:

DECIDING TO PRAISE GOD INSTEAD OF STRIVING TO PLEASE OTHERS SHOWS GOD OUR WILLINGNESS TO FOLLOW HIS PLAN.

When we show our willingness to God, He uses our seemingly simple lives to accomplish great things for His glory. Remember God's promise to Hagar through the angel that visited her in the desert? Hagar may not have seen the complete fulfillment of God's promises, but God was faithful to bless Ishmael and his descendants, just as He said. In this same way, Leah opened the door to be used by God in a mighty way when she offered praise to Him upon the birth of Judah. Let's jump ahead several years and take a peek at the fruit of Leah's obedience.

Judah, your brothers will praise you. You will grasp your enemies by the neck. All your relatives will bow before you. Judah, my son, is a young lion that has finished eating its prey. Like a lion he crouches and lies down; like a lioness—who dares to rouse him? **The scepter will not depart from Judah, nor the ruler's staff from his descendants, until the coming of the one to whom it belongs, the one whom all nations will honor** *(Genesis 49;8-10 NLT, emphasis mine).*

Judah, along with his brothers, would go on to become the foundation of the twelve tribes of Israel. As Joseph lay dying at the age of 110, he prophesied over each of his sons. The Scripture verses above are the words Joseph spoke over his son Judah. The scepter represents the lineage of kings of Israel who would come from the tribe of Judah. "From David until the Herods, a prince of Judah was head over Israel. The promise was that Israel would keep this scepter until Shiloh comes."[10]

However, the prophecy doesn't stop there. The ending of the sentence in verse 10 describes the single most important moment in history—the event that defines our very existence and eternal future. "...the one whom all nations will honor." These words refer to the coming Messiah, Jesus Christ, the King above all kings who would one day provide the way of salvation for all mankind.

Jesus would come from the tribe of Judah, the son born to Leah, some 1,600 years later.

The Attention Misconception

Throughout history, women have battled with our inner-desire for attention. From the time we are young, we crave it. If you need proof, just look at our social media feeds! We share things with others in our circles then watch to see how much approval we receive in the form of likes, pins, or shares. I for one have let the temptation for social media attention lure me into a place of self-pity and comparison. In discussions with other women on this topic, many agree that social media is one of the main ways we compare ourselves to other women.

So why do we struggle with this insatiable need to draw attention our direction?

I do not profess to be an expert in psychology. I certainly don't have all the answers, but I can dispel a widely assumed myth here. Many believe our grown-up need for attention is somehow linked to not receiving enough as a child. Though this may be true for some, I can personally declare this is not always the case. I was blessed as a child to have attentive parents. My mom and dad supported me in all my endeavors, no matter how wacky they seemed at the time.

Yet in spite of their encouragement and parenting efforts, I still let the enemy of comparison alter my self-view. The reason can be found in Paul's words to the church at Thessalonica:

"For we know, brothers and sisters *loved by God*, that he has chosen you…" (1 Thessalonians 1:4 NIV, emphasis mine).

I knew my parents loved me. I knew my friends loved me. What I didn't grasp was the magnitude of this short, powerful verse. We are *loved by God*. Once I internalized this truth, my need for attention was satisfied.

Now don't get me wrong, I still appreciate encouragement from others. I beam when my momma tells me how proud she is of me. I swoon when my husband says he would marry me all over again. I still love attention from my family and friends, but the difference now is this—I know where to find my worth, my value.

It isn't found in the number of likes on the screen.

It isn't found in the number of followers in my feed.

It isn't found in a comment, share, or smiley-face emoji.

I find the truth of who I am in God's love for me, which He showed by creating me unlike anyone else. And with that love comes the ability to push aside comparing and shine the real essence of our beauty from within, regardless of our outfits or the color of our hair. This is why we see Standard's beauty as something unattainable. It took a while, but I finally figured her out. I shouldn't have been looking to her and measuring myself. I needed to instead look to the traits Paul spoke of in Colossians 3:12, "compassion, kindness, humility, gentleness, and patience." That's the source of our sparkle.

Beauty from deep inside—something Leah found as well. But could she hold on to this new-found wisdom? Or would Leah give in to comparison with Rachel once again? In the next chapter we will make another important discovery in conquering the temptation to compare.

First, let's take some time to reflect on what we learned from Leah's experiences with the Questions for Reflection below.

CHAPTER 4 QUESTIONS FOR REFLECTION

1. CAN YOU RECALL A TIME IN YOUR LIFE WHEN YOU FELT LOVED LESS THAN SOMEONE ELSE? What words would you use to describe your feelings at that time?

   w/ Kaitlyn & the attention she got. w/ mark's family.

2. WHAT IS ONE THING YOU LEARNED FROM THIS LESSON ABOUT SEEKING ATTENTION FROM OTHERS?

   It won't give me peace. shallowness to get their attention.

3. READ THE FOLLOWING SCRIPTURE. "Therefore, as God's chosen people, holy and dearly loved, clothe yourselves with compassion, kindness, humility, gentleness, and patience" (Col 3:12 NIV). Why do you think Paul encourages us as believers to exhibit these character traits? *Never diminish and are attractive to others and bring God Glory.*

4. WHY DO YOU THINK GOD CHOSE TO BLESS JUDAH? What is one way God has blessed you recently? Jot down your answer in your journal or notes. *B/c Leah understood. His name reflects that, God uses these moments.*

5. OUR FAITH STATEMENT FOR CHAPTER 4 IS: *DECIDING TO PRAISE GOD INSTEAD OF STRIVING TO PLEASE OTHERS SHOWS GOD OUR WILLINGNESS TO FOLLOW HIS PLAN.* Take a moment today to think about this statement. How might you praise God today? How will praising God with more intention affect your daily life?

CHAPTER 5

Stay Outta My Territory

*"All adventures, especially into
new territory, are scary."*
SALLY RIDE

I GREW UP IN A COZY HOME WITH THREE BEDROOMS—one for my parents, one for my older sister, and one for me. It was nice having my own space, a quiet sanctuary to which I could retreat and spend time in solitude listening to David Cassidy records. I enjoyed my alone time, but sometimes it was just plain boring.

One day the boredom got the best of me. My sister and I put our creative minds together and devised a plan. If we shared a room, we could use the other space as a playroom. Sheer brilliance! My mother tried to talk us out of it, but eventually conceded. I think she knew full well what was on the horizon for our new idea.

We moved furniture, arranging our new bedroom to maximize the space for both of us. Then came the masking tape right down the middle. She was always stepping on my side! Sure, I stepped on her side too, but that was because I needed to borrow her hairbrush. Of course, I had to sneak to get it because borrowing items from the opponent's side was strictly forbidden. I wasn't about to lend her my records either! It didn't take long for us to realize this wasn't such a great plan after all. Sharing a room meant I only had *half* as much area to myself and zero privacy.

With an all-knowing grin, my mom helped us move things back where they started. And once again David Cassidy was all mine.

ANOTHER TRIP INTO THE DESERT

In chapter two we discovered Hagar made her second trip into the desert because of her frustrations with her circumstances. Although God was faithful to show His grace and mercy to Hagar the first time, she still allowed her focus to fall back on Sarah once again. I've been there a time or two, myself. OK, maybe three.

Have you been in that place? For me, it happens something like this:

One morning I will wake up victorious, singing God's praises for all to hear. The next moment I let my circumstances overwhelm me, and the victory is lost. My quick attention shift leaves me feeling guilty for not holding onto God's promises. I want so much to maintain steadfast trust in Him, but daily difficulties send my emotions into a tailspin!

This is why I can totally relate to why Hagar relapsed. It was as if she forgot all about God speaking to her the first time. *Oh how I understand, Hagar.*

As we enter the next chapter in the book of Genesis, we see Leah dealt with this shortcoming as well. Leah made another "trip into the desert" of her own. She faltered as soon as she let her focus turn to Rachel.

"When Rachel saw that she wasn't having any children for Jacob, she became *jealous of her sister*. She pleaded with

Jacob, 'Give me children, or I'll die!'" (Gen 30:1 NLT, emphasis mine.)

Leah wasn't the only one struggling with jealousy and comparison. Rachel was desperate to have a child, but instead of running to God with her request, she went straight to Jacob. When he reminded her it wasn't his ability to give her children but God's, she took control. We love being in control, don't we girls?

"So Rachel gave her servant, Bilhah, to Jacob as a wife, and he slept with her. Bilhah became pregnant and presented him with a son … Then Bilhah became pregnant again and gave Jacob a second son" (Gen 30:4, 7).

This familiar tune from history is being played again, sort of like my David Cassidy record. We've seen this decision to take control before. Control and comparison often work together seamlessly to infiltrate our hearts. Once we see someone else with something we want, we find a way to make it happen, even if it's not God's plan for us. The state of Rachel's heart became crystal clear in her proclamation following the birth of Bilhah's second son, Naphtali.

"Rachel named him Naphtali, for she said, 'I have struggled hard with my sister, and I'm winning!'" (Gen 30:8).

And so the game began. Point for point, Leah and Rachel tried to keep up with one another. Match per match, what one girl did, the other would follow. If you've ever watched a closely played one-on-one video game between two teenage boys, you might have an idea of the back-and-forth battle going on between these two women. According to Rachel's words, there can only be one winner. This means there will also be one loser, and Leah was not about to concede.

"Meanwhile, Leah realized that she wasn't getting pregnant anymore, so she took her servant, Zilpah, and gave her to Jacob as a wife" (Gen 30:9).

After Rachel's handmaid had two sons, Dan and Naphtali, Leah's handmaid also bore two sons, Gad and Asher. Circumstances couldn't be any more even between these two. After the birth of the second son Asher, Leah uttered these telling words in the next verse, "What joy is mine! Now the *other women* will celebrate with me."

Where is her concern? Who is she trying to please? The other women.

Is this the same woman from our last chapter who learned to praise God instead of striving to please others? Indeed it is. But we've also discovered how easy it is to lose focus on God when the hard places of life distract us. Leah was no longer concerned with giving God the glory for her blessings. She was more concerned with gaining attention from her peers. I can identify with this need for acceptance in a big way.

Accepted or Rejected?

My need for acceptance, which I shared in our previous chapter, grew even stronger in college. I went to the same grade school from kindergarten all the way through graduation, so I never had to be the new kid. I never had to make new friends. College presented a different set of relationship challenges. I would have to find peers who would welcome me into their group. My insatiable desire to be part of something led me down an uncertain path early on.

I remember one occasion when rejection hit hard. I met a few nice girls attending the same university and living in the same dorm. They were having such an easy time making new friends. From the day of freshman orientation, they'd clicked, and suddenly their group was formed.

We all took a certain class together that was particularly challenging. If you didn't study for this professor's tests, forget it! Passing would be out of the question. For that reason, many times kids got together in study groups to cram the night before a big test. I recall coming into the dorm after work one night and stopping by a certain girl's room to ask a question about the exam. When she opened the door, there on the floor sat several girls from my class. I wasn't invited to the study session.

My heart tightened and felt as though it sank deep into my stomach. I forced a smile on my face, but tears formed just beneath the surface. My head pounded. I wanted so much to be included, to be accepted.

I went to my deserted dorm room and studied by myself.

How often we lose sight of our self-worth because of what someone else thinks or says. Looking back now, I'm sure the girls in my class meant no harm to me at all, and most likely it was just an oversight or miscommunication. I did have to work, after all. If I had gone to my room, spent time in prayer and reading what God's Word said about me as His special child, my perspective would have been quite different. So would my time in college for that matter. I was not a Christian at that time, and I didn't know where to find the help my heart longed for. Now, I can re-center my focus by rejoicing in how God sees me and how He created me.

"So since we find ourselves fashioned into all these excellently formed and marvelously functioning parts in Christ's body, let's just go ahead and be what we were made to be, without enviously or pridefully comparing ourselves with each other, or trying to be something we aren't" (Rom 12:5-6 MSG).

I learned a valuable lesson through my decision to follow God and know Him more by reading His message. My worth is found in God alone. His opinion of me is the only one that matters, and that's more than enough.

BARTERING WITH BITTERNESS

Several years have passed since Jacob married Leah and Rachel. They now have eight children between them. The foundation of their problems comes to light during harvest season when Reuben, Leah's firstborn, finds some mandrakes in a field.

Now, I don't want to get into a lot of detail here about the purpose of the mandrakes and what they represent. That will lead us too far off the path, and we need to stay focused on the bitterness that has grown between Leah and Rachel. It might also make me blush. *Ahem.* However, for more information and further study on the story of the mandrakes, you can follow the link I've provided for you at the end of this chapter. This bonus material is available for those who would like to venture further into the stories of these two historic women.

For our purposes, we only need to know that both women strongly desired those mandrakes. Leah's son found them, and Rachel asked for some. When the two began to barter, Leah's resentful attitude emerged.

"But Leah angrily replied, 'Wasn't it enough that you stole my husband? Now will you steal my son's mandrakes, too?'" (Gen. 30:15).

And the truth comes out. The Bible tells us in Luke 6:45 that "... out of the abundance of the heart his mouth speaks" (NKJV). Even after this many years, Leah still harbored a grudge against Rachel. Why? Because in her mind and heart, Rachel stole her husband. How painful it must have been for Leah to hold this much anger inside for so long. Bitterness ate away at her, leaving her more and more vulnerable to attacks on her self-worth.

The drive to compare can consume us. It creates distance between us and God. Before we know it, a chasm forms. The only way to return to Him is to fully release the acidity built up in our spirits and ask Him to wash us clean. Only then can we move forward into His plan for our lives.

Neither Leah nor Rachel was ready to give God control. Both women continued letting their emotions direct their decisions. After Leah had two more sons, Issachar and Zebulun, she gave birth to her final child, a little girl named Dinah. Rachel bore two sons as well, Joseph and Benjamin.

From Competing to Agreeing

Jacob had worked for Laban twenty years.[11] He had followed God's leading when he came to this land, and he faithfully served his uncle until God told him it was time to return to his homeland.

"Then the Lord said to Jacob, 'Return to the land of your father and grandfather and to your relatives there, and I will be with you'" (Gen 31:3).

As we discovered when Leah and Rachel were still having children, twenty years is a long time to carry around hostility toward your sister. However, twenty years also gives plenty of time to grow and mature. Jacob called his two wives together to tell them what the angel in his dream told him to do. The angel said, "Now get ready and leave this country and return to the land of your birth" (Gen. 31:13b).

When the two women responded together, a great transformation took place.

"Rachel and Leah responded, 'That's fine with us! We won't inherit any of our father's wealth anyway. He has reduced our rights to those of foreign women. And after he sold us, he wasted the money you paid him for us. All the wealth God has given you from our father legally belongs to us and our children. So go ahead and do whatever God has told you'" (Gen 31:14-16).

This is the first time recorded in Scripture that Leah and Rachel agreed on anything! In their united answer, we see the words *we* and *us* used five times. The sisters finally understood the constant competition has gotten them nowhere, which brings us to our faith statement for this chapter:

SHARING OUR SPACE DOUBLES OUR TERRITORY.

Our hearts' desire for God to enlarge our territory is birthed inside us when we give our lives fully to Him. Once God radically changes us, we want nothing more than to share God's redeeming love with others! The larger the area, the more opportunity to share. Jabez expressed this so perfectly in his prayer:

"He was the one who prayed to the God of Israel, 'Oh, that you would bless me and expand my territory! Please be with me in all that I do, and keep me from all trouble and pain!' And God granted him his request" (1 Chronicles 4:10).

That becomes the cry of our hearts—an ever-increasing chance to tell others what a difference Jesus made in our lives.

Time to get right down to it. God wants to give us this land.[12] He desires to bless us, but He also desires our obedience. If we fight against one another, our efforts to spread His love will be fruitless. By cooperating instead of clashing, we open our lives to God's blessings.

I feel the need to interject a disclaimer at this point in our lesson from Leah. I am in no way condoning two women being married to the same man. I don't want to unknowingly mislead anyone reading this book. Some of us may be more familiar with the customs in the Old Testament than others. Having more than one wife was common practice in those days. So, let's not get sidetracked with Jacob's decision to marry Rachel after Leah. We still have more to discover from their story. Learning to let go of their differences set them all on a monumental course. After following God's command, He appeared again to Jacob and gave him the name Israel.[13] Not only that, but Jacob received confirmation of God's promise for enlarged territory. And what a large territory it was!

"Then God said, 'I am El-Shaddai—God Almighty. Be fruitful and multiply. You will become a great nation, even many nations. Kings will be among your descendants! And I will give you the land I once gave to Abraham and Isaac.

Yes, I will give it to you and your descendants after you'"
(Gen 35:11-12).

Wow! Leah's struggle taught us a life-changing lesson.
Working together for God's glory increases our reach. God
used Leah, Rachel, and Jacob to establish the foundation
of Israel, God's chosen people. The patriarchs of the twelve
tribes of Israel were now in place.

Common Ground

As our journey with Leah comes to a close, I'd like to share
what my friend and fellow-writer Abby McDonald has to say
about comparison. Abby's post, "What We Really Do When
We Compare," clearly captures the essence of this chapter.
I know you will feel gripped by her words as much as I do:

*The shouts echo from the family room and as much as
I try to avoid them, I know I'll have to referee. I can't see
what's taking place, but I know. My rising blood pressure
is a sure sign.*

*As I stand in the doorway, my suspicions are confirmed.
There are hundreds of toys strewn across the house,
but my three-year-old wants the one his big brother is
playing with.*

*It doesn't matter that the airplane is missing a wheel
and a fin. The reason he wants it is quite simple. His
brother has it.*

*As I kneel down before his tiny frame and try to reason
with him, mustering as much calm as I can, I can see
how I'm going to have to divert his attention elsewhere.
But to divert a determined, strong-willed child's focus
is no easy task.*

Every mom goes through it: the stage of "mine." Everything has the "mine" title and there is no discernment about it. If the child sees it, it is his.

And am I so different? Sure, I do a better job of controlling my fits of anger and masking symptoms, but the jealousy and coveting still threaten to overtake me when I don't guard my heart and mind.

Often, my gauge for how well I'm doing is comparison to others in a similar role. I look at what they have. I take mental notes on the goals they've achieved.

When I think they're moving forward at a quicker pace than I am or are more in the spotlight than I am, the flesh often takes over. What about me, God? Haven't I been faithful? Didn't I do what you asked me to do?

It isn't that I don't want them to be blessed or see their dreams realized. I know how hard they've worked. I've witnessed the sweat and the tears firsthand.

No, it's how my mind distorts their progress. I see their success as somehow taking away from my movement forward. I take my eyes off my ultimate goal, Christ, and instead begin running down a rabbit trail of discouragement and self-defeat.

The truth is, when I compare I am resurrecting my old, dead self. I am saying my new identity in Him isn't enough. That I would rather be a clone of someone else.

But friends, God doesn't create clones. He creates unique masterpieces.

Paul knew the temptation to resurrect that old self. But he also knew the power of the One who was working in him. He would not achieve full transformation in this life, but he kept pressing ahead, not looking at what was behind or in the other lane.

I want to know Christ—yes to know the power of the resurrection and participation in his sufferings, becoming like him in his death … Not that I have already attained all this, or have already arrived at my goal, but I press on to take hold of that for which Christ took hold of me (Philippians 3:10-12 NIV).

To take hold of that for which Christ took hold of me. Friends, there is nothing more than this. It is perfect love, unblemished by the world. It is everything.

Today, if you're tempted to divert from the path God has called you to and chase after someone else's dream, look up to your Author. Look up to your Finisher.

Confess with your mouth what you're feeling. He already knows.

Praise Him for the work He will finish in you. He's not done yet.

And then wrap yourself in the grace of knowing that even when we lose our focus, He's right there to pick us back up.

Rip Off the Masking Tape

If you have small children at home, you will most likely identify with Abby's story. You may even recall your own memories of sibling squabbles, like the one I shared at the beginning of the chapter. I'll always remember the brief time my sister and I spent bickering over her side versus my side of the room. What I wouldn't give to have those few days back for a do-over. If we had only realized by removing the tape that divided our sides, we would've each had double. Double the records, double the hair supplies, double the blessings.

Leah learned to remove the masking tape before it was too late. She chose not to spend the rest of her life in competition, but to embrace God's plan for her. The future she gained from that choice became more than she ever imagined possible. Only with God.

As we conclude this chapter and say goodbye to Leah and Rachel for now, let's resolve to make that choice today. God has a great future planned for us. Let's share it together and see what happens, shall we? Below are the discussion questions for review and contemplation. I pray these questions will guide your heart and mind, preparing you for the next steps along this path. Respond to them in your journal before moving on to chapter 6, where we will boldly take those next steps.

CHAPTER 5 QUESTIONS FOR REFLECTION

1. IS THERE A TIME IN YOUR LIFE WHEN YOU FELT LIKE YOU WERE IN COMPETITION WITH SOMEONE ELSE? Write down three words to describe how you felt at that time.

2. THINK ABOUT ONE THING YOU LEARNED FROM LEAH'S STORY. Record your thoughts in your journal.

3. READ AGAIN ROMANS 12:6 IN THE MESSAGE VERSION.

   "So since we find ourselves fashioned into all these excellently formed and marvelously functioning parts in Christ's body, let's just go ahead and be what we were made to be, without enviously or pridefully comparing ourselves with each other, or trying to be something we aren't" (Rom 12:5-6 MSG).

   According to this Scripture, how does God see us? What specific instruction does Paul give us here?

4. WHEN LEAH AND RACHEL CHOSE TO AGREE INSTEAD OF COMPETE, WHAT DID GOD DO?

5. OUR FAITH STATEMENT FOR THIS CHAPTER IS: SHARING OUR SPACE DOUBLES OUR TERRITORY. Take a moment to reflect on this statement. In what ways can you choose to share your space, starting today? How might this change affect your life?

Follow this link to access the bonus material for this chapter: ***www.morethanyourself.com/bonus-material***

CHAPTER 6

COOPERATION OVER COMPARISON

"You doubt your value. Don't run from who you are."
ASLAN TO LUCY, *THE VOYAGE OF THE DAWN TREADER*

I AM SO PROUD OF OUR GIRL LEAH. She came a long way from the first day we met her. Remember that meek young lady? The one with no sparkle in her eyes? Now that she set out on a purposeful journey with her husband and children, we can see more than just sparkle. We see determination and boldness bursting through.

In this chapter, we will look at three practical steps Leah took in her life to break free from comparison and move into her God-given future. But before we explore these steps, let's review our faith statements we learned from Leah's experiences.

 1. DECIDING TO PRAISE GOD INSTEAD OF STRIVING TO PLEASE OTHERS SHOWS OUR WILLINGNESS TO FOLLOW HIS PLAN.

 2. SHARING OUR SPACE DOUBLES OUR TERRITORY.

Leah knew God had her future mapped out. He also had a great plan for each of her children—her *blessings*. I can't help but wonder how things may have been different if Leah had ignored those negative voices from the beginning—the ones always comparing her to Rachel? Would she have focused so intently on winning Jacob's affections? Finding our value in affirmation from others only leads to unfulfilled longing in our spirits. Yet there's something so real we experience when we get attention—a feeling of belonging, of being loved.

Unlovable

This desire to be loved leads us to our first action step:

Step one: Find your worth in God's words.

One of my all-time favorite children's stories is *Unlovable*, a book by author Dan Yaccarino. *Unlovable* tells the tale of a not-so-cute puppy named Alfred who is told every day by his fellow pets that no one could ever love him. The cat, goldfish, and parrot all chime in with comments.

"Alfred tried his best to ignore the remarks, but it was difficult, especially since the cat had taught the parrot to say, 'Unlovable! Squawk! Unlovable!' whenever Alfred walked by. The goldfish gurgled in agreement."[14]

Their negative words are hurtful yet convincing. So much in fact that when Rex, the new neighbor dog, moves in next door, Alfred claims to be a golden retriever. He fears if his new friend knows the truth, he wouldn't love Alfred for who he is. In a heartwarming twist, Rex turns out to be a puppy that looks just like Alfred. The two become the best of buddies because Rex likes Alfred just the way he is.

I read that endearing story to my son many times in his preschool years. And even though he is now a teenager, the theme of the book still resonates with me. So many times we make the mistake of letting others determine our worth. We feel undervalued, unimportant. We can change this habit by internalizing the truth of 1 John 4:16:

"We know how much God loves us, and we have put our trust in his love. God is love, and all who live in love live in God, and God lives in them."

This short Scripture is packed full of life-changing promises! In order to grasp every point, let's break it down and look at each promise one at a time.

NUMBER ONE: *God loves us.* Amen! We could stop right there and have everything we need. But John goes on to drive the words even deeper.

NUMBER TWO: *We put our trust in God's love.* This is a tough one sometimes. We want so much to trust Him, but self-doubt threatens to undermine our thoughts. We must stay assured of God's love for us. It is unwavering.

NUMBER THREE: *God is love.* We have proof of His amazing love through the gift He gave to us— His Son Jesus Christ.

NUMBER FOUR: *When we live in love, we live in God, and He lives in us.*

If I live in God and He lives in me, I have no right to let hurtful words or actions determine my value. I also have no right to turn to other people for affirmation. God's words about me are my DNA. They describe every intricate detail of my being. They are where I find my worth.

"For you created my inmost being; you knit me together in my mother's womb" (Psalm 139:13 NIV).

Finding our worth in God's words for us and about us is the first lesson Leah learned in setting herself on a course free from comparison. We too can take this step today, letting God renew our thoughts and restore our hearts. We discover our greatest potential in Him.

Unfathomable

In the beginning, Leah understood her blessings came from the Lord, but she did not know her own worth. Her comment after Reuben was born confirms this.

"The Lord has noticed my misery ..." (29:31a).

However, the ending to her statement gives us a strong sense of the emptiness in her heart—an emptiness she thinks only Jacob's love can fill.

"... and now my husband will love me" (29:31b).

Leah was chasing the love of a man, but Someone else was chasing *her* at the same time.

Throughout the years, I've worked with pre-teen girls as a teacher and mentor. I've watched many young ladies assess their significance based on attention from boys. The pattern is always the same. If a boy is showing interest, I can see a noticeable difference in her mood. Her countenance changes. There's a bounce in her step. But when his attention fades or turns to someone else, her happiness shifts to despair. I recognize that shift because I've been there. My heart aches for her. If the cycle of emotions doesn't change, she will continue the downward spiral of misplaced value. Every woman, young and old, needs to have a moment like Leah did—a moment when we realize *who* we should be chasing.

In the book *Magnetic*, Lynn Cowell explains how this pattern looked in her own life as a teen. I love how she shares encouragement from her own personal experience:

Back in my own "wish I were dating" days, my highs and lows depended on whether or not I saw him in the hall;

my happiness was determined by whether or not he noticed me. The crush I had was crushing me.

I wish there had been someone who could have helped me. Although maybe I wouldn't have listened. But I wish someone could have shown me that the longing in my heart pointed not to my need for a guy, but to my deeper need for something even greater. That I was created to be loved perfectly and unconditionally, made to have my heart filled each and every day with love from the Perfect Man, Jesus.[15]

Lynn's book is an excellent resource for teen girls who desire a deeper relationship with the One who loves them most. She also illustrates an important point here: God created us to be loved.

We are designed to desire love. The problem is, when we don't know about the unconditional love our Savior has for us, we misplace this desire. Our longing for affection becomes a driving need to get attention from a man. This isn't fair to us, and it isn't fair to men. The pressure we put on our boyfriends or husbands to fulfill this insatiable need will ultimately end in a failed relationship.

In other words, I'm not designed to seek happiness through my husband, but rather to discover joy through Jesus.

Joy has steadfast power that will last beyond our earthly relationships. This everlasting joy can only come from God, the One whose love for us is unfathomable. This brings us to step number two:

Step two: Let praise over-rule your plans.

The Merriam-Webster online dictionary defines praise as "spoken or written words about the good qualities of someone or something: an expression of approval for someone or something: an expression of thanks to or love and respect for God." When we lift praises to God, we are expressing our approval and thanks to Him. Praising God means we understand the blessings came from Him. Praise is acknowledging the source of the blessings.

Once again we should recognize that Leah certainly understood the source of her blessings. She confessed her appreciation to God out loud for all to hear. However, Leah contradicted herself when she chose to use the blessing for her own purposes. Her plans cancelled out her praise.

"The Lord heard that I was unloved and has given me another son" (Gen. 29:33b).

"Surely this time my husband will feel affection for me, since I have given him three sons!" (Gen. 29:34b).

By accepting the blessing and then shifting her focus to what she wanted to gain, Leah unknowingly redirected the amazing plans God prepared just for her. No one else on earth could fulfill this call the way Leah could, but she doubted herself. Little did she know that God was waiting for her to give all the praise and honor to Him, so He could work through her and her children to establish Israel—God's chosen people.

Let's think for a moment about the variety of gifts God bestows upon His children. Sometimes the gift is in the form of a child, like it was with Leah. Other times, our gifts come in the form of talents or callings. Sometimes our gifts are situations—or places—where God puts us to fill a specific need. Gifts could also be finances to use for building His kingdom and sharing the love of Jesus with others.

Whatever the gifts, we often do exactly what Leah did. Oh, that's right. We can't be too hard on our sweet Leah. Have you ever taken control of a gift God gave you and tried to formulate your own plan?

Maybe you're a teacher, but you refused to take a certain position offered to you because it seemed too difficult or out of your comfort zone.

Maybe you're a writer, but you are finding your value in the number of people who read your work rather than allowing God to bring the right readers to you.

God may have gifted you for leadership, but you are avoiding getting too involved in church because you've been hurt by others in ministry—and you don't want to go through that heartache again.

You may even be a student who God called to be a light in your school, but you fear what other students might say about you if you speak out as a Christian.

Whatever the gift, it's not our place to use it for personal gain. Part of being a good gift-receiver is understanding the source. But we must also let the Gift-giver have complete control of the gift's purpose.

Writer and blogger Tiffany Parry addresses this point clearly in a post titled, "Has What You Love Lost Its Luster?" In her post, Tiffany says:

Using God's gifts for our gain rather than His glory is a recipe for resentment, not adoration.

She goes on to describe how we feel about the gifts God has given us, and what can happen when we take control...

Grace turns our have-to into a get-to. When we wrestle with our gifts and force them to do what we want them to, rather than what God intended them for, we risk falling out of love. We no longer see our calling as an anointed offering (a get-to), but as a ball and chain (a have-to). When we inevitably don't meet our own "have-to" standards we're met with guilt and shame—the polar opposite of grace and the graveyard for spiritual fruit. If what you once loved has suddenly grown claws and is tearing at your time and attention, perhaps you've forgotten the balm of grace. A little grace goes a long way...

God has a plan behind every blessing. Can He trust us with it? Let's take Tiffany's advice above and refuse to force our gifts to do what we want them to. Let's let grace turn our *have-to* back into a *get-to*. Only God knows the true potential of the gift, and we will never see it unless we let Him have the lead role in our lives.

Who Do I See Staring Back at Me?

Ask any of my former students and you will find out a fun fact about me: I am a huge *Chronicles of Narnia* fan. I even had a stuffed Aslan who kept watch over my classroom, choosing special students to sit with each day. The most recent movie installment of this popular book series by C. S. Lewis, *Voyage of the Dawn Treader*, tells the story of the young Pevensie children going on a quest to save Narnia, their former home.

In this metaphorical tale, Lucy—along with her brother Edmund and cousin Eustace—set sail on the majestic ship for the voyage of a lifetime. Along the way, shadows of doubt try to cast negativity and defeat into the hearts of the young warriors.

In one scene, Lucy expresses her inner desire to be like her beautiful older sister, Susan. Lucy rises from her bed in the middle of the night to look into a magical mirror in the hopes her wish will come true. As she gazes at herself in the mirror, a transformation takes place. She sees Susan instead of her own reflection.

Lucy is drawn into an imaginary scenario where only her sister Susan and her brothers exist—a world where she *is* her sister. When she realizes what she has done, she begins to have second thoughts. She tells her brothers she wants to return to Narnia. Edmund's next words show the magnitude of her decision.

"Narnia? Where on earth is Narnia?"

Lucy is then whisked back to her place in front of the mirror, but this time Aslan is standing by her side. Their conversation further emphasizes her need to be content with herself...

Lucy: "I just wanted to be beautiful like Susan. That's all."

Aslan: "You wished yourself away, and with it much more. Your brothers and sister wouldn't know Narnia without you, Lucy. You discovered it first, remember?"

Lucy: "I'm so sorry."

Aslan: "You doubt your value. Don't run from who you are."

Aslan represents the Voice of Truth in Lucy's life. He is a symbol for the One who gave us our gifts and expects us to use them to fulfill the great call He has on our lives.

Lucy also learned another important lesson through her time in front of the mirror. With Lucy's desire to be like someone else, she saw how empty their world would be if she didn't embrace who God created her to be. This brings us to our third and final step.

Step three: Choose to cooperate.

Lucy and her siblings each had their own special talents. Each one had a unique role to play in rescuing Narnia, but they accomplished more by working together.

Time for a little straightforward sharing. Sometimes working together with other women can be downright difficult. However, it can also bring great joy and satisfaction. God created us to be a community, but different personalities make cooperating with others a challenge! It takes work, and we need to be willing to do our part.

I shared in a previous chapter about my time as team leader and the gratification I found in embracing working with the women on my team. Let me be clear, though— we each had very different personalities. Not one of us was like the other, which made for some interesting team meetings! There were times when we left meetings without getting anything accomplished. Oh but there were other times when our gifts meshed perfectly together, resulting in great achievements for our group. Above all, we knew God put us together to build each other up and work toward our common goal. Our years together were so successful because of our commitment to teamwork. We chose to cooperate, and God blessed our efforts.

Leah and Rachel finally chose to cooperate, as well. When the two sisters agreed together for the benefit of their families and futures, a remarkable thing happened. God honored their faithfulness, just as His Word says.

"Understand therefore, that the Lord your God is indeed God. He is the faithful God who keeps his covenant for a thousand generations and lavishes his unfailing love on those who love him and obey his commands" (Deuteronomy 7:9 NLT).

What gift are you trying to control today?

Have you let your own plans over-rule your praise?

Has God put you in a place to cooperate, but you are refusing to join in?

If any of these actions hinder you from finding contentment today, let the words of the Scripture above soothe your longing soul. God is ready to lavish His love on you. Will you commit today to release comparison and obey His commands for your life? Leah did, and it made all the difference.

I'm sad to say we've come to the end of our time with Leah. I feel like we've gotten to know her as a friend. I pray her story will stay with us long after we close this chapter. Her life was important, and yours is too.

Below are ten Scriptures for reference during those times when we feel someone else is loved more than we are. They reaffirm the truth about who we are and how God feels about us. Let's allow these verses to minister to our hearts in a new and freeing way. We will experience a breakthrough with God's Word as our guide.

TEN SCRIPTURES FOR WHEN YOU FEEL UNLOVED:

1. "See, I have written your name *on the palms of my hands*" (Isaiah 49:16a).

2. "We know how much God loves *us, and we have put our trust in his love. God is love, and all who live in love live in God, and God lives in them*" (I John 4:16).

3. "For we are God's masterpiece. He *has created us anew in Christ Jesus, so we can do the good things he planned for us long ago*" (Ephesians 2:10).

4. "Don't you realize that your body *is the temple of the Holy Spirit, who lives in you and was given to you by God? You do not belong to yourself …*" (1 Corinthians 6:19).

5. "Since God chose you to be *the holy people he loves, you must clothe yourselves with tenderhearted mercy, kindness, humility, gentleness, and patience*" (Colossians 3:12).

6. "We know, dear brothers and sisters, *that God loves you and has chosen you to be his own people*" (1 Thessalonians 1:4).

7. "So now there is no condemnation *for those who belong to Christ Jesus*" (Romans 8:1).

8. "For the Lord your God is *living among you. He is a mighty savior. He will take delight in you with gladness. With his love, he will calm all your fears. He will rejoice over you with joyful songs*" (Zephaniah 3:17).

9. "See how very much our Father *loves us, for he calls us his children, and that is what we are! But the people who belong to this world don't recognize that we are God's children because they don't know him" (1 John 3:1).*

10. "Don't be afraid, for I am *with you. Don't be discouraged, for I am your God. I will strengthen you and help you. I will hold you up with my victorious right hand" (Isaiah 41:10).*

PART 3

BLESSED MORE

All in Favor, Say *I*.

"Never change who you are so that others will like you. Just be yourself and the right people will love you just for being you."
NAKAYLA, AGE 12

As we begin our conversation about our third and final precious woman of God, I have to pause for a moment to thank you all for walking beside me on this journey. I feel like we've become fast friends, because we all share similar life experiences. In the same way, I feel we've connected with these women in Scripture who meant so much to God that their stories were recorded for us. Their place in history was established so we could identify with their trials and rejoice over their victories. The next woman I'd like to introduce is no exception. Her name is Hannah.

While uncovering the story of Hannah, I couldn't help but wonder if she and I would've been friends had we lived in the same period in time. Scripture doesn't reveal anything about Hannah's childhood. In fact, we don't learn about her until after her marriage to a man named Elkanah. We meet them at the beginning of the book of 1 Samuel, around 1000-1100 B.C.[16]

Elkanah was a Levite. Remember Levi from part two? Levi was one of Leah and Jacob's sons. Levi and all his brothers grew to become the foundations of the twelve tribes of Israel. The Levites were a blessed group, set apart and chosen because of their loyalty.[17] Elkanah came from the house of Kohathites, known as the most honorable of the Levite tribe.[18]

"Elkanah had two wives, Hannah and Peninnah. Peninnah had children, but Hannah did not" (1 Sam. 1:2 NLT).

You may be thinking, "Oh no, we've heard this before." And without a doubt, you would be right to consider this. Here we have two women once again living in the same family, and the author of 1 Samuel wastes no time pointing out a distinct difference between the two. From what we've learned so far, we may be tempted to assume where this is headed. However, something unique sets Hannah apart from the women we've met before.

> *Year after year this man went up from his town to worship and sacrifice to the Lord Almighty at Shiloh, where Hophni and Phinehas, the two sons of Eli, were priests of the Lord. Whenever the day came for Elkanah to sacrifice, he would give portions of the meat to his wife Peninnah and to all her sons and daughters. But to Hannah he gave a double portion* **because he loved her, and the Lord had closed her womb** *(1 Sam. 1:3-5 NIV, Emphasis mine).*

Two important truths become clear right from the beginning. Elkanah loved Hannah deeply. He demonstrated this love by giving her a double portion each time the family worshiped at the temple. Secondly, God allowed Hannah's infertility.

DOES GOD REALLY DO THINGS LIKE THAT?

If you've experienced infertility like Hannah, you know the pain and longing she felt. You try over and over, wondering whether or not you will finally have the joy of a beautiful child to call your own, only to sink into disappointment once again when the results come back. Wanting to quit, you press on thinking maybe next time will be different. On top of this roller coaster of emotions, you also question how much planning is too much. Theological concerns flood your anxious thoughts. *Is it right to use medical methods to increase our chances? Are we taking control away from God if we undergo fertility treatments? Will God understand?*

Only a person who has been through it can truly empathize with the thoughts above. I've been there myself. For six long years my husband and I tried to conceive before our son was born, so I know the anguish Hannah felt.

Your battle may not have been with infertility; maybe yours was something entirely different. Health problems, financial crisis, emotional turmoil, and countless other challenges plague our world. I can say with all certainty each and every one of us has experienced personal affliction or a difficult circumstance at some point in our lives. Most likely more than just one or two. Like me, you may have asked this question:

WHY DOES GOD ALLOW BAD THINGS TO HAPPEN?

God's Word clearly emphasizes that we live in a fallen world. And because of the presence of sin, we will have hardships.

"I have said these things to you, that in me you may have peace. In the world you will have tribulation. But take heart; I have overcome the world" (John 16:33 ESV).

However, there have also been times when God allowed an affliction in someone's life for the greater purpose of establishing His kingdom. A perfect example is a man who became instrumental in building new churches and proclaiming the love of Jesus Christ. His words still bring comfort and hope to the world today. We know him as Paul.

A Painful Perspective Change

Paul happens to be one of my all-time favorite historical figures. Paul never shied away from the chance to share how Jesus changed his life. Prison couldn't even stand in the way of Paul describing his faith to anyone who would listen, and even some who wouldn't. Talk about boldness! How I would love to be so consumed with grace that I would speak about Jesus with brave determination like Paul did.

Oh, but Paul wasn't always that way. In his former life he was the known persecutor of Christians, and he had no intention of believing in this *Jesus character*. It took a radical transformation of the God-kind to make him into the energetic preacher and church planter he became. And that transformation came with serious physical injury.

As he (Paul) was approaching Damascus on this mission, a light from heaven suddenly shone down around him. He fell to the ground and heard a voice saying to him, "Saul! Saul! Why are you persecuting me?" "Who are you, lord?" Saul asked. And the voice replied, "I am Jesus, the one you are persecuting! Now get up and go into the city, and you will be told what you must do." The men with Saul stood speechless, for they heard the sound of someone's voice but saw no one! Saul picked himself up off the ground, but when he opened his eyes he was blind. So his companions led him by the hand to Damascus (Acts 9:4-8).

Saul's blindness lasted three days, and during that time

God worked in his heart to change him into the man God needed him to become. Those three days were undoubtedly filled with pain, uncertainty, and fear, but Saul prayed and waited for an answer. His response came in the form of an obedient man by the name of Ananias. Ananias followed God's totally unorthodox command to visit this known hater and lay hands on Saul, so he would regain his sight.[19] God had big plans for Saul. From that day on he would be known as Paul, the great evangelist.

PAIN COMES IN DIFFERENT FORMS

Through this story we can see God wanted to get Paul's attention. Paul's statement in 2 Corinthians 12:9 further confirms God's hand in his life and the reason for Paul's sufferings:

"Each time he said, 'My grace is all you need. My power works best in weakness.' So now I am glad to boast about my weaknesses, so that the power of Christ can work through me."

God had a definite purpose for Paul. Is it possible God had special plans for Hannah, as well? Could her affliction have been part of a greater design? We will find the answers to these questions in time, my sweet friends. But let's remember—something is holding Hannah back from embracing her full potential. Just like Leah and Hagar, Hannah did not enjoy her life because she saw a woman who had something she desperately wanted. This comparison fueled her sorrow.

Leah felt as though Rachel was *loved* more than her.

Hagar felt as though Sarah was *noticed* more than her.

Hannah believed Penninah was *blessed* more than her. This can be the most painful comparison of them all.

"But her rival wife taunted her cruelly, rubbing it in and never letting her forget that God had not given her children" (1 Sam. 1:6 MSG).

Ouch.

The pain of harsh words stings much worse than physical pain. It lasts much longer, too. Hannah not only had the heartbreak of no children to call her own, but she also endured the destructive words Penninah so often poured out. It may seem as though circumstances couldn't get much worse for Hannah, but from the deepest valleys come the most important lessons. From Hannah's valley, we find our faith statement for this chapter:

 ### HARDSHIP PREPARES THE HEART.

Without hardships we would not receive the joy that comes from answered prayers and miracle moments. Sometimes hardships will come and go quickly. Other times, those hardships will last much longer. Peninnah taunted Hannah with cruel words for several years.

"Year after year it was the same—Peninnah would taunt Hannah as they went to the Tabernacle. Each time, Hannah would be reduced to tears and would not even eat" (1 Sam. 1:7 NLT).

In her distraught state, Hannah likely didn't even notice her husband Elkanah's attempts to console her. He loved her whether she had children or not, and he wanted his love to be enough to satisfy her.

"'Why are you crying, Hannah?' Elkanah would ask. 'Why aren't you eating? Why be downhearted just because you have no children? You have me—isn't that better than having ten sons?'" (1 Sam. 1:8 NLT).

Elkanah's attempts went unnoticed by Hannah, but Peninnah's constant put-downs did not. Mean-spirited talk has a way of doing that—making us feel less than our true value.

GETTING PERSONAL ABOUT PENINNAH

Though our focus throughout this chapter remains on Hannah, it wouldn't be right to pass over Peninnah without trying to understand her actions. She isn't mentioned much in this biblical account, but there is still a lot to glean from what is said about her.

Allow me to open my past and be candid with you right now. I identify with Peninnah. Those who know me personally now would never think I could ever say a hurtful word about another person, but I wasn't always the person I am today. Like many adolescents, I fumbled through a time of uncertainty and low self-esteem early in my teen years. Though temporary, my inner-struggles led me down a confusing path.

Junior high can be a treacherous time for kids—each one trying to discover who she is and determine her own identity. I was no exception. During this process however, I decided that putting on a tough exterior would somehow shield me from any potential rejection. As a result, I tried my hand at being a *mean girl,* hurling insults and leaving hurt feelings in my dust.

I'm ashamed of the fake persona I created way back then, and I grieve inside just thinking about it. Thankfully, through grace we can let go of shame and know God has forgiven us of the mistakes from our pasts. He also makes a way for us to use past mistakes to help others today.

Looking back at my choices helps me understand people who choose to be mean. Revisiting those old feelings equips me to see what lies beneath the surface of the hard outer-shell some choose to wear.

For the majority of my adult life, God has given me the opportunity to teach pre-teens in a variety of settings. Sunday school, dance classes, and public school have all provided a backdrop for my time with kids. How cool is that? And with this honor also came the chance to show them how to be kind, how to encourage others, and how to be a blessing. My principal and boss once said to me, "I bet you were the most well-behaved student in school." If he only knew! There's no doubt in my mind where my desire to teach originated. It came straight from my failures, because through my weakness, God's strength is revealed. I thank God every day for the chance to mentor young people and say life-giving words that will lift them up to reach their full potential.

Poor Peninnah

Peninnah wore a hard shell, too. Her criticism of Hannah most likely stemmed from seeing that double portion heaped on Hannah's plate each year, knowing Elkanah loved Hannah more. I'm not making excuses for her behavior, but understanding the cause of her resentment helps us empathize with her hurts.

When I counsel young people who are being targeted with hurtful comments, I emphasize the need to understand the reason behind the words. There are many reasons why someone would choose to be mean, but the root cause is most often a deep seed of insecurity that she just doesn't know how to process. Make no mistake—this type of behavior should not be tolerated. However, answering bitter words with more bitterness only worsens the problem.

Hannah provides a shining example of how to handle mean girls. Take a look at her actions immediately following the passage where we learned how poorly Peninnah treated Hannah.

"Once when they had finished eating and drinking in Shiloh, Hannah stood up" (1 Sam. 1:9 NIV).

STAND UP

Imagine with me that day in the temple—the day that repeated itself every year of Hannah's married life. With all reverence Elkanah led his family there, to this holy place where the priests lived. As they gathered around the table to eat, Elkanah pledged his forever love to Hannah while Peninnah cast hateful glares her way, hoping to make eye contact. Hannah didn't flinch or utter a sound, but on this particular occasion, she'd had enough. While each member of the family remained seated, Hannah stood up right in the middle of the meal.

It was time for her to take a stand. She knew exactly what to do—Hannah prayed.

"In her deep anguish Hannah prayed to the Lord, weeping bitterly" (1 Sam. 1:10 NIV).

In Ephesians chapter 6, our mighty warrior Paul wrote a letter teaching the church at Ephesus about how to stand firm during hard circumstances. Verse 13 instructs, "Therefore put on the full armor of God, so that when the day of evil comes, you may be able to stand your ground, and after you have done everything, to stand."

Standing symbolizes our determination to trust God with our issues and cast our cares on Him.[20] This posture also says we are ready for God to work in our situations. In Hannah's day, praying could be done kneeling, lying prostrate, or standing. Hannah's choice to stand at the table and walk confidently through the entrance to the tabernacle signified her readiness to give it all to God. The prayer she recited aloud revealed a Paul-style of boldness which can only come from the Holy Spirit.

"Then she made a vow: 'Oh, God-of-the-Angel-Armies, if you'll take a good, hard look at my pain, if you'll quit neglecting me and go into action for me by giving me a son, I'll give him completely, unreservedly to you. I'll set him apart for a life of holy discipline'" (1 Sam. 1:11 MSG).

Wow, our girl Hannah doesn't hold back! What a power-packed prayer she proclaimed that day. I'll let you in on a little secret, too. God loves powerful prayers. Hannah was well on her way to throwing comparison aside and trusting God with her future. She came to a turning point, one we've seen before through Leah and Hagar. She began focusing on God instead of others.

What happened next shows us evidence of her humble spirit and gentle nature.

"As she was praying to the Lord, Eli watched her. Seeing her lips moving but hearing no sound, he thought she had been drinking" (1 Sam. 1:12 NLT).

It seems odd that Eli's natural inclination would be to assume Hannah had been drinking. This was the temple. Wouldn't people normally come there to pray? Shouldn't he be used to seeing this type of thing?

We need to realize Eli may have encountered other women in the temple quite frequently—women who, shall we say, didn't have Hannah's good intentions. This town was full of hurting people, just like our world today. Eli possibly faced people with alcohol addiction and other problems on a daily basis. In fact, his two sons, Hophni and Phinehas, were not without blemish. (For further study on Eli's sons, visit the link at the end of this chapter to download the bonus material.)

Whatever the cause of his accusation, Hannah's response is priceless. I wish I had her composure. What a kind-hearted lady she was!

"'Oh no, sir!' she replied. 'I haven't been drinking wine or anything stronger. But I am very discouraged, and I was pouring out my heart to the Lord. Don't think I am a wicked woman! For I have been praying out of great anguish and sorrow'" (1 Sam. 1:15-16 NLT).

Matthew Henry's commentary puts it this way. "When Eli rebuked Hannah, she didn't return censure for censure by telling him he needed to look at home at what his own sons were doing. She guarded her mouth and responded graciously and with proper respect."[21] Hannah's grace under the pressure of false accusations is something we should all strive to achieve. And if you've ever been accused of something you were not guilty of, you know how difficult this can be.

In our home, we want our son to learn how to respond in a Christ-like way to the grumpy grown-ups in his life. We have been blessed to raise our son in a community where his teachers, coaches, and church leaders have poured encouragement into him and given him a solid foundation of good character. However, as much as we'd like to think every adult he comes in contact with will treat him with kindness, the reality remains that at times he will face uncomfortable confrontations. This life-lesson has become more and more crucial in high school, as he is developing his independence one step at a time. Learning early how to handle these moments will make it easier for him in the future when he is out from under our protective roof.

When this book is released, our son will be finishing his tenth year of school. This momma's not quite ready for all that independence yet, but I want *him* to be ready when the time comes for him to leave home. Our growing young man has shown incredible respect and restraint in answering back when I lose my cool (temporarily, of course). Because quite honestly, sometimes I'm the grumpy grown-up he has to deal with!

I hope he will continue to learn from Hannah's example and react with grace when others accuse him of something he didn't do or lash out at him in frustration. In my opinion, he is definitely on the right track. But we could all use a reminder from time to time, and helping our children learn this tough lesson can serve as a refresher course for us as well. Here are a few practical steps that will help us remember how to respond, not retaliate, when we feel falsely accused.

1. COMMUNICATE WITH COURAGE. We always strive to teach respect in our home. Growing up in the south, both my husband and I learned early to honor our elders. We chose to pass on this same lesson to our kids. When children are young, I believe it is appropriate to answer with "Yes, sir" or "Yes, ma'am" when talking to trusted adults. As our son grows older, we have also seen occasions where he needs to follow up with an explanation. We shouldn't try to cover our actions with an excuse, but sometimes it's OK to explain yourself, if done the right way. Notice in the passage above Hannah was quick to point out to Eli that she had not been drinking, but was pouring out her heart to God. Explaining herself helped Eli realize the truth. Her heartfelt speech gave way to understanding. In my son's case, he may likely face situations with high school teachers, college professors, or future employers, when he needs to clear up a misunderstanding. We want him to feel free to communicate with his teachers and address things appropriately. It takes courage to talk it out, but sometimes—like in Hannah's case—explaining a misunderstanding is necessary.

2. REPLY WITH RESPECTFUL WORDS AND TONE. Notice in verse 16, Hannah refers to herself as Eli's maidservant, "Do not consider your maidservant a wicked woman"

(NKJV). A maidservant is another word for a female slave or handmaid.[22] By using this word to describe herself, Hannah accepted Eli's authority and established her willingness to serve. This humility softened Eli's heart and broke down any barrier that would prevent him from hearing what she had to say.

3.   **Gratitude goes a long way.**

"'In that case,'" Eli said, 'go in peace! May the God of Israel grant the request you have asked of him.' 'Oh, thank you, sir!' she exclaimed." (1 Sam. 1:17, 18a).

Hannah's courage to communicate and respectful reply prepared Eli to receive her words. Once he knew her true reason for entering God's presence that day, he made a remarkable proclamation. He assured Hannah of God's intent to grant her request for a son! Her immediate reply was an act of gratitude. "Thank you." Those two simple words speak appreciation and acceptance. Hannah accepted Eli's bold message from God and continued their encounter in an attitude of grace.

No more.

Hannah carried Eli's words from God in her heart as she left the temple that day. She had every intention of claiming her victory and receiving her blessing.

"Then she went her way and ate something, and her face was no longer downcast" (v. 18b NIV).

I cannot count the number of times I've dropped to my knees, cried out in anguish to God and released a burden to Him. I would then feel that peace only He can give and know without a doubt He would answer my prayer. Walking away in joyous victory, I would soon let the cares of the world cause me to question. I would allow doubt-filled thoughts to steal my triumph and send me spiraling back to where I began.

Through our study of Hagar and Leah, I learned I'm not alone in this conflict. These ladies struggled too! But when I introduced you to our sister Hannah, I told you there was something different about her, and now we've reached a defining moment. Hannah threw away her downcast countenance once and for all. She was over it.

Merriam-Webster's dictionary defines "downcast" as not happy, confident, or hopeful. Psalm 43:5 of the New International Version states:

"Why, my soul, are you downcast? Why so disturbed within me? Put your hope in God, for I will yet praise him, my Savior and my God."

So, we can conclude that the opposite of downcast is *hopeful*. Hannah had hope—a hope that would carry her through a momentous time in her life. A hope that would keep her focused on God and His promise. A hope that would help her honor the commitment she made to the Lord in her powerful prayer.

As soon as Hannah replaced her sadness with everlasting hope, we do not find another word mentioned about Peninnah or her taunting words. She fades into the background of the narrative, so we can see Hannah's devotion to God's plan through an unbelievable vow at the temple. A vow unlike any other recorded in the Bible, and quite possibly the hardest decision a mother has ever had to make.

CHAPTER 7 QUESTIONS FOR REFLECTION

1. DO YOU KNOW SOMEONE WHO APPEARS TO ALWAYS HAVE EVERYTHING GO RIGHT FOR THEM? A person who seems to always be blessed and rarely experiences hardship? Take a moment to pray for this person. Thank God for blessing her, and ask for God's peace through her difficult times.

2. THINK OF A TIME SOMEONE SPOKE HARMFUL WORDS TO YOU—WORDS OF CRITICISM, PUT-DOWNS, OR JUDGMENT. What did we learn through Peninnah's story that can help us understand the hurt that person may have been feeling? Take a moment to pray for this person, as well. Ask God to help you release any hurtful words and move forward with *His* Word.

3. OUR FAITH STATEMENT FOR THIS CHAPTER IS: *HARDSHIP PREPARES THE HEART.* What hardship have you experienced that God used (or is using) to prepare you for a blessing in your own life?

4. REFLECT ON GOD'S PROMISE TO HANNAH IN VERSE 17. Read this verse as a promise from God to you personally. After reading it, describe in one sentence how God feels about you right now. Write it down in your journal.

5. WHEN HANNAH RELEASED HER COMPARISON ONCE AND FOR ALL, SHE TURNED FROM DOWNCAST TO HOPEFUL. What is your definition of hope?

6. BRAINSTORM THINGS YOU CAN DO EACH DAY TO MAINTAIN A HOPE-FILLED ATTITUDE.

Follow this link to find the bonus lesson on Hophni and Phinehas: ***www.morethanyourself.com/bonus-material***

REMEMBER ME?

"A noble friend is the best gift."
C. S. LEWIS, *THE LAST BATTLE*

SHE SPOKE WITH THE CONVICTION OF SOMEONE WHO KNEW the urgency of the moment. Her words sought out my worried spirit. All the while, she looked intently into my eyes as she grasped the opportunity we'd both been given this fateful Sunday. Little did I know she would be leaving me to spend eternity with Jesus just a few short days later.

Renee always knew how to seize the moment. Growing up with several health problems, Renee's grandmother claimed her as a true miracle from God when she was a young child. The doctors did not expect her to survive, but she did. And throughout her young life she relied on God and trusted Him for one miracle after another in her body. God faithfully showed Himself at work in her life, and she never failed to testify of God's goodness to everyone she knew.

Because of her health issues, she couldn't have a child through natural means. But Renee and her husband sowed into the lives of many children through foster care. When the opportunity came for them to become parents to a special young boy, once again Renee did not let the chance pass by. Her dream of motherhood was fulfilled as God orchestrated this special family and placed them together for a unique purpose.

Renee and I came to know one another as moms in the same church family and soon discovered all we had in common. God bound us together through similar experiences and children the same age. When my husband and I became pastors, she stepped right alongside me. We needed someone to fill the role of children's director, and she willingly raised her hand. Just another example of her go-getter attitude.

We considered ourselves partners in ministry and sisters in life. We were always together! Rounding up kids for their Wednesday night Bible classes, shopping trips to purchase supplies for church, or planning adventures, we trotted along in perfect sync. I couldn't imagine spending one day without talking to her. We were the best of friends.

Throughout adulthood Renee continued to visit the doctor on a regular basis, doing her best to be a good steward while trusting God with her healing. Sometimes I could see the look of exhaustion on her face, but even on bad days, nothing stopped her from arriving early and staying late. If she said she would do something, I could count on it.

That's why I knew this day—this conversation—held such importance.

Though weak and weary from dialysis, she did not want to miss the chance God was giving us both as we sat on the front row together before Sunday service. I leaned in with my arm around her. She looked at me with deep sincerity. Renee told me three things I will never forget—how much she appreciated all I had done for her, I was the best friend she'd ever known, and she loved me.

I knew then this time was a gift from God. We needed to share our feelings, bare our hearts, and leave nothing unsaid.

In turn, I told her I loved her dearly and would always be there for her family. I went on to reassure her that whatever small deeds I had done, she had returned to me more than tenfold. The conversation continued for just a few moments more, but the tears and sentiments we shared brought a sense of completion for us both.

Renee passed away the next Sunday.

The lesson I learned from her that day changed my life. Captured opportunities culminate into a life without regrets. If we walk daily in the Spirit, we can be confident God will prompt us when He leads us straight into an opportunity. Our job is to seize it.

Renee reminded me so much of Hannah. Both women endured hardships. Both were committed to God's plan. Both also understood the importance of their roles as moms. Even though Renee's time as a mom was short, God no doubt placed her in that position for a reason. Her relationship with her son will prove paramount as God continues to reveal His ultimate plan.

Like Renee, Hannah's time as Samuel's mother would be shorter than any mom would hope for, but no less significant. Through her obedience and making the most of an opportunity, Hannah would soon understand her God-given purpose.

Let's continue our visit with Hannah and watch as she makes this amazing discovery.

CONTINUING TO STAND

"and in due time she gave birth to a son. She named him Samuel, for she said, 'I asked the Lord for him'" (1 Sam. 1:20 NLT).

Eli said it. Hannah believed it. God did it. Hannah received the fulfillment of the promise made by God. She conceived and gave birth to Samuel. Now, things start to get tough.

Start to get tough? Hasn't Hannah had enough hardship already?

Yes, our dear Hannah had her fair share of turmoil dealing with Peninnah all those years. Once she decided to stand and let God prepare her heart, she symbolically put on her blinders. Hannah chose not to give in to the voice of comparison.

Yet how many times have we resolved to take a stand, only to face even more difficult times? Just because we make a firm commitment doesn't mean we won't have any more hardship. In fact, sometimes it only gets harder. Why? Because God desires to see us grow deeper in our knowledge of Him.

Hannah made a serious commitment to God at the temple. Since that time, Peninnah hasn't even been mentioned. This could indicate one of two possibilities. Either Peninnah had a radical change of heart (it could happen), or Hannah is continuing to stand. Now that Samuel rested in her loving arms, her faithfulness and determination would be tested.

"The next year Elkanah and his family went on their annual trip to offer a sacrifice to the Lord and to keep his vow. But Hannah did not go. She told her husband, 'Wait until the boy is weaned. Then I will take him to the Tabernacle and leave him there with the Lord permanently'" (1 Sam. 1:21-22).

Permanently.

From our perspective today, this seems a bit extreme. So allow me for a moment to take us back to our faith statement from chapter two:

Focusing my gaze on God reveals my child's true worth.

In her time spent worshipping at the Tabernacle, Hannah renewed her focus on God. God began revealing His plans for both Hannah and Samuel. If Hannah refused to listen, this plan would not be fulfilled. She knew this, and we find further confirmation in the rest of her conversation with Elkanah at the end of this verse.

"'Whatever you think is best,' Elkanah agreed. 'Stay here for now, and may the Lord help you keep your promise.' So she stayed home and nursed the boy until he was weaned."

I can only imagine the look on Elkanah's face as he heard Hannah's directive! This exchange reminds me of the many times my husband has caught me in one of those moments. Some of these moments happen when I get frustrated with an untidy home. My challenge goes something like this:

"No one is leaving this house until it's spotless!"

And my all-knowing husband responds, "Whatever you think is best, honey." He's so sweet, and always knows what to say.

Husbands learn from years of experience how to identify when their wives are in this zone, but the discussion between Hannah and Elkanah was much more than that. Hannah's conviction from the Holy Spirit showed through her countenance. Her words held authority. Elkanah deferred to her obvious wisdom. She was a woman who had spent time in prayer—deep prayer—and her closeness to God could be felt by those around her.

I want so much to be like that. Don't you?

I want to be so close to God that when people look at me, they see Him. I want to be so deep in His Word that people seek me out for advice. I want to be so in touch with the Holy Spirit that others notice a visible difference in my life. Ephesians 4:2 teaches us to be "completely humble and gentle; be patient, bearing with one another in love."[23] By following this command, we can be like Hannah. We can be so focused on God that He reaches others through us.

There is something else worth mentioning here. Although Hannah holds firm in her resolve to return Samuel to the Tabernacle, she never loses sight of her current role. Hannah's job is to stay home and nurse her son. She spends every day nurturing Samuel—being his mom. She doesn't try to tackle other tasks. She doesn't question whether her sacrifice is worth it. She doesn't waste time wishing for another assignment.

Hannah knew the power in following God's call, even if it seemed trivial and thankless in the midst of it.

We find strength in accepting where God has us, for each season of life brims with purpose. Fully embracing each day, even the monotonous ones, means we are relying on God's promises. So whether you are a stay-at-home mom, working full-time, or both, live today as if everything you do is for a specific purpose—because it is, my friend. It is.

CURING SHORT-TERM MEMORY LOSS

"When the child was weaned, Hannah took him to the Tabernacle in Shiloh. They brought along a three-year-old bull for the sacrifice and a basket of flour and some wine.

After sacrificing the bull, they brought the boy to Eli. 'Sir, do you remember me?' Hannah asked. 'I am the very woman who stood here several years ago praying to the Lord.'" (1 Sam. 1:24-26).

My precious mother-in-law writes everything down. For as long as I can remember, I picture her sitting in her chair under the dim light of the side table lamp, penning the events of the day. She writes about who comes to visit, the weather, phone calls received, and anything else that reminds her of God's goodness in her life. At ninety years old, she still journals every single day. She also keeps her journals, so she can remember.

From her example I have discovered the benefits of writing things down. Some refer to this as a prayer journal—a place to write down our prayers and record how God responds to those prayers. Before I began journaling, I had a hard time remembering all God had done in my life—the miracles, the changes, the answers. Writing things down cures this short-term memory loss. In fact, in *20 Ways to Improve Your Memory*, an article by psychology expert Kendra Cherry, writing things down is noted as an important tool for boosting memory.[24]

That annoying comparison monster would love for us to forget God's blessings and begin looking at others with envy. Hannah gives a great demonstration on how to remember, which brings us to our faith statement for this chapter:

 WE QUIET THE UNWELCOME VOICE OF COMPARISON BY REMINDING OURSELVES OF GOD'S GOODNESS.

I adore Hannah's enthusiasm in this Scripture as she approached Eli! I imagine her eyes wide, wanting to take him back to that memory not so long ago when they both experienced God's presence in such a real way. It was as if she was saying, "Don't you remember, Eli? We stood right in this very spot when it happened! You and I both saw and heard what God did. Wasn't it marvelous?"

She went on telling Eli more about the developments since that magnificent day …

"I asked the Lord to give me this boy, and he has granted my request. Now I am giving him to the Lord, and he will belong to the Lord his whole life" (1 Sam. 1:28a).

Have you ever received wonderful news, and you couldn't wait to share it with someone? The kind of news that made you want to call a special person right away, just so they could rejoice with you? Hannah received the best news of all in the form of a baby boy, but she had to wait a few years to share this incredible report with Eli. She knew he would be the one to appreciate it the most. After all, God used him to speak the prophecy of Samuel's birth. Now the time had come. Bursting with anticipation, she told Eli the good news. And as the person who would appreciate it most, Eli praised God with her.

"And they worshiped the Lord there" (1 Sam. 1:28b).

As Hannah gave her only son Samuel back to God, she should have been heartbroken. I know I would have been, for sure. But Hannah pressed through potential feelings of worry, fear, and heartbreak. She let go of the what-ifs and uncertainty about the future. She placed herself in an attitude of rejoicing, thanksgiving, and praise. Remember our faith statement from chapter four? Hannah was all over it.

Deciding to praise God instead of striving to please others shows God our willingness to follow His plan.

When we show our willingness to follow His plan, miraculous things happen. Hannah was no exception.

MORE THAN A PRAYER

Just as Hannah anticipated sharing her story with Eli, I have been eager to share this part of Hannah's story with you. I've been waiting for it since we began talking about her, and now the time has come.

The good news. The big moment.

Hannah prayed, but it was more than a prayer. I've included my favorite version of Hannah's prayer here for you. Think of Hannah as we read her words. Picture her act of praise. Listen to her, crying out from her heart.

> *"My heart rejoices in the Lord;*
> *My horn is exalted in the Lord.*
> *I smile at my enemies,*
> *Because I rejoice in Your salvation.*
> *No one is holy like the Lord,*
> *For there is none besides You,*
> *Nor is there any rock like our God.*
> *Talk no more so very proudly;*
> *Let no arrogance come from your mouth,*
> *For the Lord is the God of knowledge;*
> *And by Him actions are weighed.*

The bows of the mighty men are broken,
And those who stumbled are girded with strength.
Those who were full have hired themselves out for bread,
And the hungry have ceased to hunger.
Even the barren has borne seven,
And she who has many children has become feeble.
The Lord kills and makes alive;
He brings down to the grave and brings up.
The Lord makes poor and makes rich;
He brings low and lifts up.
He raises the poor from the dust
And lifts the beggar from the ash heap,
To set them among princes
And make them inherit the throne of glory.
For the pillars of the earth are the Lord's,
And He has set the world upon them.
He will guard the feet of His saints,
But the wicked shall be silent in darkness.
For by strength no man shall prevail.
The adversaries of the Lord shall be broken in pieces;
From heaven He will thunder against them.
The Lord will judge the ends of the earth.
He will give strength to His king,
And exalt the horn of His anointed."
(1 Sam. 2:1-10 NKJV)

What boldness! What connection to God! This prayer outlines the intricate details of God's intentions for Hannah. In other words, it explains why she needed to be Samuel's mom in the first place.

The messages we can glean from her poignant prayer will deepen our faith even more. However, if I'm not careful, I will veer off track. (I've been known to do that a time or two.) So in order to stay focused on the message of this book, we will jump straight to the final verse. If you would like to study more of Hannah's prayer, simply visit our private page via the link at the end of this chapter. I've included bonus material for further study on Hannah's famous prayer. It's just one small way I can show my appreciation to you.

A Powerful End

"He will give strength to *His king*, and exalt the horn of *His anointed*" (v. 10, emphasis mine).

To comprehend the depth of Hannah's final sentence, we must first take a peek back in time. God chose Israel as His people, and His plan included ruling over them. For that reason, Israel was governed by judges appointed by God. Israel had no king.

"In those days, Israel had no king; all the people did whatever seemed right in their own eyes" (Judges 21:25).

So if Israel had no king during this time period, who could Hannah have been referring to when she said *His king* and *His anointed*? God had big plans for Samuel, bigger than any of the people there could have imagined. Hannah's prayer hinted at that plan in a grand statement for us all.

Samuel would be God's agent for establishing kingship in Israel.

In his article *Israel Gets a King*, Bob Deffinbaugh says, "The birth of Samuel, much like the birth of John the Baptist, was a divine initiative whereby God's silence was broken."[25] Hannah had no way of knowing one day Samuel would grow up to appoint his two sons judges over Israel. Unfortunately, they didn't do such a stellar job. The people rejected them. This detail caused the elders of Israel to request a king. They wanted to be like everyone else.

"Then all the elders of Israel gathered together and came to Samuel at Ramah, and said to him, 'Look, you are old, and your sons do not walk in your ways. Now make us a king to judge us like all the nations'" (1 Sam. 8:4-5).

Though God grieved at their request, He instructed Samuel to give the Israelites what they wanted. You will find more about this historical turning point in the book of 1 Samuel, chapters 8 and 9. Through a series of events, God brought a dashing man named Saul and Samuel together. Saul then became the first king of Israel.

Even though Saul was first, he is not the king spoken about in Hannah's declaration. You see, there was another who would be called a man after God's own heart. The man Samuel would one day seek out from the family of Jesse and anoint as the future king of Israel—the shepherd boy, David.

"But God removed Saul and replaced him with David, a man about whom God said, 'I have found David son of Jesse, a man after my own heart. He will do everything I want him to do'" (Acts 13:22).

As Hannah's prayer came to a close, her words made a powerful claim. She was not just praying *to* God, but also speaking a word of prophecy *from* God. Matthew Henry's commentary says, "This prophecy may refer more immediately to the government of Israel by Samuel, and by David whom he was employed to anoint."[26]

Oh, but it gets even better. Hannah may also have been

prophesying about the King above all kings—Jesus, the Son of God, who would be born through the lineage of David to come to earth and save the world.

"We have reason to think that this prophecy looks further, to the kingdom of Christ, and the administration of that kingdom of grace, of which she now comes to speak ... The ancient expositors, both Jewish and Christian, make it to look beyond David to the Son of David."[27]

Hannah's act of obedience and following through with her commitment opened the door for God to use her to fulfill His plan for the salvation of all mankind.

I'd say her job was pretty important. Yes indeed.

Who Would've Thought?

I wonder if Hannah ever looked at Peninnah's life and felt blessed less than she was. I wonder if she doubted whether or not she heard God right. Did she ever see what other women had and question her value? Did she hold her one and only son and question why her time with him would end so soon? Of course she did, which is why we can relate to her—as a woman, as a mom, as a chosen child of God.

We all doubt. We all have times when we feel less than someone else. But right now I pray we all feel a shift in our perspective based on this revelation from Hannah's life story. Hannah thought the gift God gave her, Samuel, was the fulfillment of what God wanted to do in her life. That would have been enough, but God had more.

Our view is limited to what we think the blessing will be. We have no idea what God has in store for us when we walk in obedience.

CHAPTER 8 QUESTIONS FOR REFLECTION

We cannot say goodbye to Hannah without highlighting three steps from her experiences to put in place in our own lives. The next chapter will be devoted to outlining those steps. Let's get ready by reviewing Hannah's story and reflect on what we learned with the questions below.

1. RECALL WHAT HANNAH ASKED GOD FOR IN 1 SAMUEL 1:9–11. How did God answer her prayer?

2. REVIEW THE FAITH STATEMENT FOR THIS CHAPTER: WE QUIET THE UNWELCOME VOICE OF COMPARISON BY REMINDING OURSELVES OF GOD'S GOODNESS. Think of a time when God answered your prayer. Jot it down in your journal. Read over it, and offer thanksgiving to Him specifically focused on that answer.

3. HANNAH DID NOT WAIVER FROM THE COMMITMENT SHE MADE TO THE LORD. In your journal, list three character traits to describe Hannah.

4. READ OVER HANNAH'S PRAYER ONCE MORE. Identify two to four lines that speak to your heart today. Record those lines in your journal.

5. HAVE YOU EVER FELT AS THOUGH YOUR POSITION OR CURRENT SITUATION WASN'T MAKING A DIFFERENCE? What did you learn from Hannah's story that will help you when those feelings arise?

6. THINK ABOUT THE MOST IMPORTANT POINT YOU LEARNED FROM HANNAH'S STORY AS IT RELATES TO YOUR OWN LIFE. Write down this key lesson in your journal. Review your answers to these questions before moving on to chapter 9.

Follow this link for more on Hannah's prayer.
www.morethanyourself.com/bonus-material

CHAPTER 9

COMMITMENT OVER COMPARISON

"Commit everything you do to the Lord. Trust Him, and He will help you."

PSALM 37:5

I SIMPLY ADORE THE THREE WOMEN WE'VE COME TO KNOW through this book. Each one is unique, yet we can identify so closely with their experiences. Hannah is a one-of-a-kind lady, no doubt about it. There's something special about her that draws me back to her story again and again, each time revealing new insight and fresh wisdom.

I've often wondered what it is about Hannah that makes her so relatable. Is it her struggles? Her perseverance? Her longing for answered prayer? Her desire to worship? These questions fueled my passion to study Hannah's life and share what I learned with you here. From Hannah's circumstances, I've formulated three final practical ways to take action when we feel compelled to compare. Before we look at these last steps in our journey, let's review the faith statements from chapters seven and eight:

 1. HARDSHIP PREPARES THE HEART.

 2. WE QUIET THE UNWELCOME VOICE OF COMPARISON BY REMINDING OURSELVES OF GOD'S GOODNESS.

Hannah oozes godly character. But these positive traits didn't come easily. Doing the right thing and maintaining the right attitude takes effort. Here are three steps we can apply in our own lives to conquer comparison once and for all. These tips, along with those learned in the previous chapters, will set us on a course to a changed, more content life.

Step 1: Worship and repeat.

"The entire family got up early the next morning and went to worship the Lord once more. Then they returned home to Ramah" (1 Sam. 1:19).

Recall with me the day Hannah cried out to the Lord, asking Him for a son. Eli told her God would grant her request, and her sadness turned to hope. God gave a promise. Hannah was well on her way to receiving her blessing. I'm sure she went to sleep full of joy that night. They had a long journey ahead of them the next morning, and I'll bet Hannah wanted to get an early start.

Yet she and her family arose extra early the next day and went to the temple. They chose to worship one more time before returning home. They worshiped the Lord *again*.

Repetition is an amazing thing.

I can remember the words to every Sunday school song I learned growing up …

"Deep and wide, deep and wide, there's a fountain growing deep and wide!"

I can remember all fifty states in alphabetical order, because my fifth grade teacher made us repeat it every day …

Alabama, Alaska, Arizona, Arkansas, California, Colorado, Connecticut ... you get the idea.

Repetition causes sticking power. Words, thoughts, and habits stick when we practice repeating them again and again. Transferring this technique to worship and verse memorization takes our relationship with God to a new level. Hannah knew this, which is why she was ready when God answered her prayer.

OVER AND OVER

During my years as a young mom, I had an ongoing problem with overwhelming worry. Not just the everyday-kind of worry, but intense worry—the kind accompanied by rapid heart rate and shakiness. I didn't know it at the time, but I suffered from anxiety attacks. Little things would set it off, and I had no idea what to do about it. I thought I would have to live with it, until I read Philippians 4:6-7:

"Do not be anxious about anything, but in every situation, by prayer and petition, with thanksgiving, present your requests to God. And the peace of God, which transcends all understanding, will guard your hearts and your minds in Christ Jesus" (NIV).

This passage seemed to be the answer I longed for, but would it be enough to put an end to my problem? I claimed this as my go-to verse. I resolved to keep focused on this specific truth long-term, not just for a quick fix. To prepare, I read these two verses over and over. Soon the day came when a serious attack hit without warning.

It was a day filled with anticipation. I had read, researched, and done my homework. Because of my extensive allergies, we had to find the right furry companion to bring into our home. I found a sweet labradoodle puppy, and we named him Teddy. He was my four-year-old's new best friend.

From day one, the stress of having a new member of the household to feed and care for sent my emotions spiraling. I couldn't get past feeling overwhelmed and anxious. I went to Philippians 4:6-7. (I thought I had memorized it, but in those anxious moments, my mind would not cooperate.) I read it. Then I read it again. And again.

I read it more times than I can even count, but soon I was able to speak it without looking at the words. My repetition made it stick. I repeated it until my heart rate began to slow and the shaking subsided. God's Word calmed my anxious thoughts and quieted my heart.

Since that day, I've held onto that verse like an innocent child with a favorite stuffed animal. I look to it for comfort. A remarkable thing happened over the years—I had fewer and fewer anxiety attacks. In fact, now those times are almost nonexistent. When an attack threatens, all I have to do is begin my go-to verse, and the feelings go away as quickly as they came.

I pray as you read on, you will accept the following words not as an admonition, but as a lesson that took me years to learn. I share it with you in the hope you will see its value in every hard situation you face.

When you don't feel like worshiping, worship once more. If you don't have time to memorize Scripture, read the verse again. Too tired to pray? Try praying again. The habit of repetition grabs us from the downward path of defeat and points us in a new direction.

I've taken ownership of several other go-to verses through my life. Maybe you have a few quotes that come to mind right now as your favorites. At the end of this chapter, you will find ten more Scriptures to carry with us as we live out God's plan each and every day. I pray you will find a few new favorites among these and add them to your arsenal.

Step 2: Be confident in who God says you are.

"My heart is confident in you, O God; my heart is confident. No wonder I can sing your praises!" (Psalm 57:7).

Confidence is a dirty word among Christians. We are taught to be humble and gentle, not confident. Confidence equals arrogance, and arrogance sends the wrong message. Yet time and time again throughout history, God's girls exuded confidence.

So what's a Jesus loving, Bible reading girl to do? The key to understanding God's definition of confidence can be found underneath the surface. We must discover where our confidence comes from and why we need it. Looking at the foundation, we may find out that being confident isn't so bad after all.

QUIET CONFIDENCE

I don't know her name. I know her only as a woman of faith who served the Lord daily with gladness and gratitude. She didn't pray for a child, but God blessed her with a son just the same. When her son became ill, she continued to trust God. Then, the unthinkable happened. Her young boy passed away. Without hesitation, she uttered the surprising words, "It will be all right."

She is referred to as the Shunamite woman, and her story is found in 2 Kings.[28] She received a miracle that day, but while I write these words my heart fills with sorrow. I am reminded of the many people in my community and circle of friends who've experienced loss, even the loss of a child. When someone we love gets sick, we don't always see a miracle manifest the way we want. So even though we can rejoice with the Shunamite woman because God breathed life back into her son, I want to focus on her perspective. By saying "It will be all right," she expressed her trust in God, regardless of the outcome. I'm truly amazed at her strength in the midst of the turmoil. Her confidence in God did not waver in the worst possible circumstance.

Hannah also displayed this same confidence. She did not know what God had in store for Samuel, yet she never turned back. I'm sure she repeated Eli's words over and over on those days when life as a stay-home mom seemed lackluster at best. "Go in peace! May the God of Israel grant the request you have asked of him." Maybe these were her go-to words when things looked bleak. Even though Hannah had no idea what the future held, her confidence in the promise remained.

Ephesians 3:12 says, "In him and through faith in him we may approach God with freedom and confidence" (NIV).

The "him" in this verse refers to Christ, in whose resurrection and promised return we have total assurance. We must make sure our confidence is not misplaced. Confidence in ourselves leads to pride, and pride takes us far away from God. Paul was an expert in this area, and God made things clear for him as we learned in chapter 7. Paul taught the churches about confidence, and from those teachings we understand how to keep it in its rightful place.

"For we who worship by the Spirit of God are the ones who are truly circumcised. We rely on what Christ Jesus has done for us. We put no confidence in human effort" (Phil 3:3).

In her book, *A Confident Heart Devotional,* Renee Swope explains how comparison attempts to rob us of the confidence we have in God. Renee writes about Eve and how Satan wanted to distract her from who she was as a child of God. She writes, "Yet Satan wants us to focus on our flaws and feelings of inadequacy, then exhaust our energy figuring out how to hide them. But we don't have to go along with his schemes. Instead we can recognize his lies, refute his temptations with truth, and focus on God's acceptance, security, and significance. Then we can thank God for His provision and His promises that remind us of who we are in Him."[29]

Remain confident in who God says you are, what He says to do, and what He has for you. Only then will you be able to release the need to measure up.

So why does God give us this confidence? Like every good gift from Him, it has a specific purpose—to do the will of God.

"Therefore do not cast away your confidence, which has great reward. For you have need of endurance, so that after you have done the will of God, you may receive the promise" (Hebrews 10:35-36 NKJV).

Let's hold onto our confidence in Christ today! God gave it to us for a reason. Now we understand its source, and when the enemy says, "Compare," we can answer back with bold faith:

"I rely on Jesus and what He has done for me!"

READY, SET, COMMIT!

A huge part of Hannah's progress involved getting her mind set on the right things. Just like a football player before the championship game, we must get our "game faces" on in order to keep focused. We have to get ourselves ready. When Hannah stood up from the table, she had her mind made up. She would not listen to harsh comments or hurtful words any more. Instead, she told herself, *I can do this.* Hannah's determination brings us to step three.

Step 3: Get your mind set, and commit.

I'll go ahead and say what we're all thinking.

Commitment is hard.

We don't like to talk about commitment because it makes us feel pressured. Truthfully, I would never pick up a book that had the word *commitment* on the cover! So I won't give you a long lecture on the importance of commitment. (I would never do that to you.) Instead, allow me to begin step three with this beautiful example of a fellow writer's journey to overcoming comparison. I believe her thoughts illustrate it perfectly.

Talented blogger Katie Williams shared this story with me about how God helped her get in the right mindset when the voice of comparison brought discouragement. Katie had listened to a teaching by speaker and life coach Lisa Allen. Lisa's training on "yardsticking" revealed something new to Katie. Yardsticking refers to "the impulse many women have to measure themselves against one another in order to determine their own social standing and self-worth."[30] Katie refers to a community of writers she joined when she felt the call to write:

I was not familiar with the term yardsticking, but I've actually been practicing this pesky habit for many years. This has recently come to light in my writing, particularly since I felt a nudging from God to pursue writing and speaking as a ministry. Although I have always had a deep love of words, this particular path is very new to me, and when I'm new to something, I tend to compare myself to others as a way to measure my calling and capability. If I feel I fall short, I am likely to convince myself God didn't really say what I thought He said, and that I'm not really cut out for the job He wants me to do.

My first post didn't garner a lot of attention, and as I found myself looking at the views and replies on other people's posts, I quickly became discouraged about my own prospects as a writer. I'm ashamed to admit I had gone from feeling good about something I had done to convincing myself that God clearly wasn't telling me to write, and that I really just needed to abandon my dream and eat a pint of Moose Tracks ice cream instead.

Fortunately, our God is good, and it turns out I was out of Moose Tracks anyway ... bummer. I quickly turned on one of my favorite songs and flipped open my Bible to Proverbs 16. This chapter features many verses about the guidance of the Lord and the power of words. Knowing I had already fallen victim to yardsticking, I also called up one of my favorite anti-discouragement verses: "My flesh and my heart may fail, but God is the strength of my heart and my portion forever" (Psalm 73:26).

With the help of the Holy Spirit, I began to realize I was unfairly comparing my posts to those of writers who have been active in the community for months. Once I figured that out, I was able to see the blessing behind the numbers that had originally intimidated me, and I found myself joyfully reading posts by other members as a way to encourage my fellow writers and to see my own unique growth opportunities. I truly am thankful for the community, and I look forward to participating in it more frequently and fearlessly in the future!

Katie went on to thank the teacher of the training session for making her more aware of the temptations and how she can fight those thoughts. Katie knows the dangers of measuring ourselves against someone else, often someone who has been on the journey longer than we have. She also knows how to get her mind set in the right zone for moving forward. She is committed to stick with God's plan and have confidence in His direction.

Oh, and Psalm 73:26 happens to be one of my favorite verses too.

Reading Katie's story, I could easily have spoken those exact words myself. I've been in that place. In an earlier chapter I bared my battles as I worked through the writing of this book. Before I began the part of pounding out the keys on my computer, I spent two years with the ideas I longed to share swirling around in my head and heart. I listened to stories, read blog posts, researched articles. I tucked them all neatly away, waiting for the day when God would say, "It's time."

Nearing the end of those two years and the beginning of the actual writing process, I began to doubt. One thing helped me push past comparing my calling to others: *Saying it out loud.*

At first, I was intimidated at the thought of telling others about the idea. Fears shot forth in record numbers.

I was afraid of people thinking I was bragging about it. "I wish she'd stop talking about that book already!"

I was afraid someone else with more experience, more friends, and more talent would have the same idea. Where would that leave my book?

I was afraid of not following through. Once I told someone about it, I had to finish it!

But I had to ignore those fears and speak it anyway. Because as we learned previously, words hold power. The more I talked about it, the more the excitement grew. Talking about the dream helped seal the commitment.

When the fear of an unfulfilled dream says "Stop," commitment beckons, "Keep going."

It hurts just a little to share these vulnerable thoughts with you, but I've also come to discover I'm not alone. As I mentioned in the introduction, women of all ages have unknowingly fallen into the comparison trap. And if I could highlight one thing I hope we will take away from this book, it would be this:

The women of the Bible felt it too. Since the beginning of sin, the enemy has been trying to discourage women and keep them from finding peace in who they are as God's chosen children. He has been relentless in this pursuit, but God has given us everything we need to put an end to his schemes today.

Are you willing to worship over and over, even when it's inconvenient?

Have you lacked the confidence that comes from God?

Are you struggling with committing to whatever God has for you?

I'm right there with you. Let's take Hannah's progress to heart today, and remember her strength and resolve as we read Psalm 37:5-6:

"Commit everything you do to the Lord. Trust him, and he will help you. He will make your innocence radiate like the dawn, and the justice of your cause will shine like the noonday sun."

Turning the page on this chapter of Hannah's life also signifies a turning point for us. God gave us great insight through the lives of Hannah, Leah, and Hagar. We could say goodbye now and be content with our newfound wisdom, ready to erase comparison and embrace God's plan. However, before we say *mission accomplished*, God wants us to take this a step further. Yes friend, there's more to the mission than we could think.

Below are ten Scriptures for when you feel blessed less than someone else. Hannah felt less-blessed because she couldn't have children. Has a prayer gone unanswered for you? Let theses verses give you peace today. Commit them to memory. Call on them when you feel *less*. Read them over again, and let them renew your weary spirit.

10 SCRIPTURES FOR WHEN YOU FEEL BLESSED LESS THAN OTHERS

1. "ALL PRAISE TO GOD, THE FATHER *of our Lord Jesus Christ, who has blessed us with every spiritual blessing in the heavenly realms because we are united with Christ"* (Ephesians 1:3).

2. "FURTHERMORE, BECAUSE WE ARE UNITED WITH *Christ, we have received an inheritance from God, for he chose us in advance, and he makes everything work out according to his plan"* (Ephesians 1:11).

3. "THE HEAVENS ARE YOURS, AND THE *earth is yours; everything in the world is yours—you created it all"* (Psalm 89:11).

4. "BLESSED IS HE WHOSE TRANSGRESSION IS *forgiven, whose sin is covered"* (Psalm 32:1 KJV).

5. "BUT EVEN IF YOU SHOULD SUFFER *for what is right, you are blessed. Do not fear their threats; do not be frightened"* (1 Peter 3:14 NIV).

6. "IF YOU FULLY OBEY THE LORD YOUR GOD *and carefully keep all his commands that I am giving you today, the Lord your God will set you high above all the nations of the world"* (Deuteronomy 28:1).

7. "AND ALL THESE BLESSINGS SHALL COME *upon you and overtake you, because you obey the voice of the Lord your God: Blessed shall you be in the city, and blessed shall you be in the country"* (Deuteronomy 28:2-3 NKJV).

8. "There is no longer Jew or *Gentile, slave or free, male and female. For you are all one in Christ Jesus*" *(Galatians 3:28).*

9. "God blesses those who are poor *and realize their need for him, for the Kingdom of Heaven is theirs*" *(Matthew 5:3).*

10. "This means that anyone who belongs *to Christ has become a new person. The old life is gone; a new life has begun!" (2 Corinthians 5:17).*

CHAPTER 10

WHAT WAITS
BEYOND THE QUEST

"Instead of conforming to the personalities and opinions of others, act and speak the way you know is right. If you're worried about what others think of you, just remember that at the end of the day, only one perspective matters—God's."

HANNAH B., AGE 12

IN THE INTRODUCTION, I MENTIONED MY MOTIVATION FOR WRITING this book. Through research and studying, I read countless articles, blog posts, status updates, and tweets expressing the struggle of comparing. Each one resonated deep within me and pulled me into an instant connection with women everywhere. But even before then, something sobering opened my eyes to the depth of this spiritual battle. Let's begin with a personal story from Brittyn:

> I was never considered popular, but I was always okay with that fact because I knew people liked me because I am nice, and I hang out with everyone. This was true until sixth grade graduation. We were told about an award that not even the teachers knew about—or who would win, anyways. The Optimist Award is an award for the "best student," meaning that you had good grades, and didn't get in trouble often, or ever for that matter. I thought even though I qualified, I would never get it because I am not a popular kid. There was one awarded to a girl and one to a boy. Everyone knew who was going

to win the boy's award. This guy was very kind and didn't get in trouble once the whole year. All the girls liked him and the teachers called on him to run errands, an overall good kid.

I was sitting in my seat all dressed up for the graduation ceremony, and I watched as this boy was handed the award. The announcer told everyone to quiet down again so that everyone could hear who would win the girl's award. I remember waiting for the most popular girl to be called, but she wasn't called. The announcer said my name into the mic. "Brittyn, please come up to accept your award." I was filled with joy as I heard my name. I jumped up out of my seat and walked up to the stage and started crying happy tears. After it was over, I felt wonderful like I was floating on clouds.

I am now confident in who I am, not because I won an award, but because I was myself. I was rewarded for being good. If every kid or adult would be themselves, the world would only get better. People would no longer have to act like someone else to have a label like popular put on them. Labels mean nothing. I know that now and I will never forget that.

When I hear young Brittyn's story, I am thankful her school recognized her for her strong character. Sometimes we receive encouragement or accolades from others, but many times we feel unnoticed—like Hagar. I can picture Brittyn sitting in the auditorium that day, and all around her are hundreds of other girls her age. Each one wonders if her name will be called. In other auditoriums everywhere sit thousands of others, looking at the girl on the right and the one on the left. Each one thinking, "When will it be my turn?"

My motivation for writing this book began with the hope that one day all girls will know the truth. They are noticed. They are loved. They are blessed.

WHAT BREAKS MY HEART

The doubts may begin there in the auditorium, but if nothing changes, each girl soon becomes the teen who determines her own worth based on being asked to the formal dance. Then she grows into the twenty-something, full of potential, who changes her mood emoticons according to her relationship status. That young lady soon becomes a brilliant woman, one who takes hold of the purpose set before her. But with a glimpse toward the woman sitting beside her, she loses focus and allows comparison to steer her off-course.

This breaks my heart.

Just as we are bombarded with unintentional comparison every day, young girls also experience this in their normal activities. Whether in the classroom, on the sports field, or during other pastimes, our girls will hear comparative comments by peers often. In a survey of one hundred seventh grade girls, fifty-five percent admitted they've heard a friend or classmate compare them to someone else. Likewise, fifty-seven percent responded they've been compared to another child by a grown up.[31] I don't mean to place blame here, but we do it all the time without even realizing it. I'm totally guilty.

"If you would study more, your grades would be as good as your friend, Sarah's. She's not smarter than you, but she puts forth more effort."

"Allison makes first chair in band every time because she practices more. If you practiced as much as her, you might make first chair sometime, too."

"Why can't you keep your room clean like your sister? If you were as organized as her, you wouldn't lose things all the time."

Even as I write the words, I feel the sting.

In the passionate words of Albert Einstein, "Everybody is a genius. But if you judge a fish by its ability to climb a tree, it will live its whole life believing it is stupid." Obviously, our first task is to prayerfully consider our words, and ask God to help us express our concerns for our kids' well-being in an encouraging way. Then, we will be ready to help them identify those innocent comments and deal with them appropriately before they stick.

"We demolish arguments and every pretension that sets itself up against the knowledge of God, and we take captive every thought to make it obedient to Christ" (2 Corinthians 10:5 NIV).

According to Paul's words in Corinthians, God gives us the authority to capture words as they enter our minds and make them obedient. In other words, we can put them in their rightful place—away from our hearts. I don't know about you, but I did not begin practicing this skill until later in life. I'm still working on it today. How amazing it will be to see the next generation of women exercise spiritual authority, blossoming into the wise women God intends for them to become!

So with that in mind, allow me to issue a challenge with one final question:

WHAT IF WE TAKE THESE TRUTHS WE LEARNED HERE AND NOT ONLY APPLY THEM TO OUR OWN LIVES, BUT SHARE THEM WITH THE NEXT GENERATION?

The potential results are mind-blowing.

Without a doubt, we would hear more stories like the one above. We would also find more advice like these wise words from young Emma Grace:

Being a thirteen-year-old girl, I've definitely compared myself before. I would compare myself to the people I want to be like, whether it be celebrities, or just girls from my school. When I compare myself I get carried away, and my mind won't be able to think about anything else but the person who I think is perfect. When that happens I have to turn straight to God. I have to remind myself that God made me in His image, not the world's image. I ask Him to forgive me for wanting to change His work of art, and I ask Him to show me how to imitate Him by being a light in a dark world. God is the only perfect thing that will ever exist, so I want to be like Him. I once heard a quote that said, "If all the flowers wanted to be like roses, then spring would lose its loveliness." So, if everyone tried to be like one perfect person, then the world would lose its uniqueness and loveliness. Instead of all of us trying to be something else, let's all try to be ourselves.

Well said, Emma Grace.

FULL CIRCLE

I hope you will take time right now to celebrate the steps we've completed. As you breathe in this last chapter, think how far we've come. Not only have we uncovered six pivotal faith statements, but we have also taken significant steps toward getting beyond comparison and putting it behind us. We've dug into stories, learned Scriptures, and had a few laughs too. Laughs are always good! However, while we do our celebratory dance, we should not think of this as a finish line we've crossed. No, our journey looks more like a relay race. I may have been the slowest girl in junior high physical education class, but I know a little bit about track. At least, I know what the track looks like.

The track is round.

Or maybe, it's oval. See? I told you I knew a *little bit* about track. The runner's track doesn't extend in a straight line from point A to point B. To run the entire length of the track, you must complete a full circle. In a relay race, another runner waits eagerly at the starting point to grab the baton from you and carry on the race. That picture is the essence of this chapter. When we learn life-changing truths, God expects us to pass those on to someone else. Who better to pass the *Over It* message to than a young woman or teen in your own life?

Maybe you have a daughter or granddaughter. Maybe a niece or friend at church comes to mind. If you do not have a personal connection such as these, that's OK! Begin praying today for God to bring to your mind someone you could pray for. Prayers will make a huge difference in a young girl's life, and your prayers may be just what she needs. The Scripture lists at the ends of each section are a perfect resource to get you started. A powerful prayer can be as easy as speaking God's Word over a person's life.

If you are a mom or grandmother with a preteen or teen girl at home, I would like to offer you additional resources on our private page for further study. Visit the link provided at the end of chapter five to find the free PDF download, *Steps to Helping My Girl Handle Comparison*. This download offers even more ideas for practical activities you can do at home.

WHAT IT MEANS TO BE CONTENT
TO BE SIMPLY YOURSELF

"But if you're content to be simply yourself, you will become more than yourself" (Luke 14:11 MSG).

The actual age comparison begins to surface in a girl's life will vary depending upon the uniqueness of individual life experiences. However, it is at that time when we become more aware of ourselves in relation to those around us. The understanding of the first part of this verse is critical.

"... if you're content to be simply yourself ..."

In the previous verse of the Message version, Jesus gave an illustration meant to serve as an example of what someone who is content to be simply herself would do in a specific situation.

"When you're invited to dinner, go and sit at the last place. Then when the host comes he may very well say, 'Friend, come up to the front.' That will give the dinner guests something to talk about!"

Jesus explained a scenario in which a dinner guest, invited to a feast, must choose where to sit in relation to the host.

Those who held a higher position in society were placed in closer proximity to the host—a place of honor. I can imagine myself in that situation now—walking in the room and feeling all eyes fix on me as my face begins to burn. Looking at the empty seats, I quickly scan the busy room to decide which one is most suited to my stature as a simple peasant. If I hesitate too long, the snickers and whispers will begin, so I quickly grab a seat in the back. Just as I settle in, happy to be invited at all, the honorable host arrives and motions toward me to come forward. He has a seat prepared especially for me—right next to him.

In a room where everyone is ranked in order of importance, it hardly seems fitting to talk about being happy with yourself. Even so, the connection is found in the transition between the two verses. Leading up to our key Scripture, Jesus says, "What I'm saying is …"

I love how Jesus always knew when His followers needed it explained a different way for clarification. I'm right there with them every time. The simpler the better, and Jesus knew how to explain in simple, understandable ways. His transition brings us to the point of what Jesus wanted His followers to take away that day, and what He wants us to take away, as well.

 ## PUTTING OTHERS BEFORE MYSELF PUTS ME IN MY PLACE NEXT TO HIM.

By being content, we are at peace with ourselves. The word *simply* used in this context means *only* ourselves. It does not refer to simplicity as it relates to the lifestyles we live—like what to wear, how we spend money, and other daily decisions. When I walk into that room, I must be at peace with myself, and thus not concerned at all with the snickers and whispers from the many other invited guests. And by understanding the place I deserve, God will make sure I am escorted to the seat He planned just for me.

ANOTHER LOOK IN THE LIGHTED VANITY MIRROR

Some time has passed since the beginning of our quest, when I took you back to a sensitive place, sitting in front of that lighted vanity mirror. I shared about my experience there in the introduction to this book. (If you're the type of person who likes to skip the introduction and get right to the good stuff, you might want to go back and read it now.)

I want to venture back there again. There's more to that story, and it's finally time for me to tell you what happened when I left the cosmetology class that day with my newfound insecurity. God had something special in mind for me. He always does. And in true God-fashion, He revealed His message in an extraordinary way.

"Why don't you just get a nose job?"

I didn't have to ponder her question for long. My thoughts turned immediately to my mother.

"Because my mom wouldn't allow it!" was my tactful response.

You see, I was right to be concerned about the reaction of a loving, supportive mother who would definitely not approve of such a thing. Remember, I was only a teen. The instructor's idea was simply not an option for me.

I knew I should have been proud of my nose. It's a family nose. My mother, my grandfather, and most likely generations before him all donned this common trait. Frankly, I felt embarrassed to tell my mom about the conversation. My nose never bothered me before. At least I thought it hadn't, until the comparison monster crept in and caused me to doubt.

After arriving home from the class, I decided to chat with my mom and her dear friend about the experience. Coincidentally, Mom's friend also has a similar nose. So much so in fact, that she and my mother were often mistaken for sisters when they were together.

"Why would you ever consider changing your nose?" Mom's wise friend asked. "It's a sign of royalty."

Royalty.

In early Victorian England, men and women with a bump atop the bridge of the nose were instantly recognized by the people. "The nose was considered the strongest, highest, and most perfect expression of character."[32] The Aquiline nose was the most highly regarded of all nose types. When you saw someone with the distinguishable bump, you knew she was of noble birth.

Now isn't that just like our loving God? Through the hurt of insecurity, He revealed my worth. In the midst of my doubt, He reminded me of my royal position as His child.

THE JOURNEY'S END?

The girl in the mirror found new freedom in her image that day. She went on to become a college graduate, a wife, a mom, a teacher, and a writer. We shared some crazy times with her, didn't we? Her short run as team leader, the dried-out enchiladas, and let's not forget those overprotective instincts through the kindergarten years! Yes, it's been a journey filled with many stops and starts, detours and missed turns, because the core struggle of comparison kept coming back to distract her. But the ultimate answer—God and His unending grace—kept calling her back to the path. What sweet, sweet grace it is.

So as she keeps moving forward in her journey, the reality is that the problem will still call to her and try to draw her into itself in that sneaky, subtle way it has. Because that's what the enemy tries to do. So when the comparison voice whispers, which path will she choose? Which will *I* choose?

Which will *you* choose?

We can once again let down our defenses and fall back into the comparison trap that tangles us. Or, we can choose contentment. We can choose cooperation. We can choose commitment to our Creator. We can delete comparison from our lives and discover the beauty right where we are. We have been made new, and now we know the secret.

"So God created human beings in his own image ..." (Genesis 1:27).

God made us in His image, and images can be seen in a reflection. So, God created us to be a reflection of Him. How could we want to change something He made with such love and care? How could we desire to be anything other than who He designed us to be?

Friends, can I share from a vulnerable place? Can I bare my heart for a moment? I fall way short of God's image. We all do. And just maybe, in all that *trying* we get a little down on ourselves, afraid we might disappoint God. We wonder how He could love someone who messes up so often and can't seem to stay on the right path. That's why the second part to the secret we now know is so important.

God made a way for us to get closer to Him through His son Jesus, who is "the exact likeness of God" (2 Corinthians 4:4).

We may fall short, but Jesus doesn't. We may fail, but Jesus' love covers us—sins and all. God knew this, way before He breathed life into any of us. He knew what we would be like, and I can't help but wonder if He smiled at the thought. Yes, I'm going to imagine He did. So even though our quest is almost over, the journey never really ends. We can take off those uncomfy sandals for a while and prop up our feet, coffee in hand, but just for a few minutes. We've been offered a challenge—not the kind that can be conquered in a day, but the kind that requires daily renewal on our part. The challenge that can be found in Ephesians 4:24:

"Put on your new nature, created to be like God—truly righteous and holy."

I love a good challenge, and this is the best one of all! Forget the sandals. I've got just the pair of shoes for the job, blue ones with bright pink laces. And when I get in position to start again, (after a nice long nap,) I'm going to think of Hagar, Leah, Hannah, and all the other beautiful women of the Bible who learned the secret to conquering comparison to live out God's plan. I'm going to think of you, too. You're joining the ranks of these amazing ladies, and as I pray for you I will be reminded of our time together:

May we welcome all God has for us each and every day as we get over the compulsion to compare. Our quest may be ending, but the journey continues.

The adventure has only begun, dear friend, and I cannot wait.

NOTES

1. MINDEL, NISSAN. "Hagar." Kehot Publication Society, Accessed June 15, 2015. *www.chabad.org/library/article_cdo/aid/112053/jewish/Hagar.htm*.

2. LOCKYER, HERBERT. *All the Women of the Bible.* Grand Rapids: Zondervan, 1988. *www.biblegateway.com/devotionals/all-women-bible/2015/11/09*

3. FLETCHER, ELIZABETH. "Hagar, Her Story." Accessed June 15, 2015 *www.womeninthebible.net/1.2.Hagar.htm*

4. DEEN, EDITH. All the Women in the Bible. New York: Harper & Row, 1955. p. 265.

5. HENRY, MATTHEW. "Genesis 21." Matthew Henry Commentary. Accessed June 10, 2015. *www.biblegateway.com*

6. MARK 15:40, MARK 16:1 NIV

7. SHIRER, PRISCILLA. *He Speaks to Me.* Chicago: Moody, 2006. p.112

8. DEEN. p. 30.

9. THOMAS, ROBERT L. "praise." *NAS Exhaustive Concordance of the Bible.* Nashville: Holman, 1981. Accessed July 1, 2015. *www.biblehub.com/hebrew/8416.htm*

10. GUZIK, DAVID. "Genesis 49." *Guzik Bible Commentary.* Accessed July 1, 2015. *www.biblehub.com/commentaries/guzik/commentaries/0419.htm*

11. WIERSBE, WARREN. "Genesis 31." *BE Bible Study Series commentary.* Accessed July 6, 2015. *www.biblegateway.com*

12. DEUTERONOMY 1:8 NLT. "Look, I am giving all this land to you! Go in and occupy it, for it is the land the Lord swore to give to your ancestors …"

13. GENESIS 35:10 NLT

14. YACCARINO, DAN. *Unlovable.* New York: Scholastic, 2001. p. 3

15. COWELL, LYNN. *Magnetic.* Colorado Springs; Multnomah, 2014. Kindle location 204.

16. BIBLE TIMELINE. Accessed July 6, 2015. *www. biblehub.com/timeline/1_samuel/1.htm*

17. BRAMER, STEPHEN. "Levite." Accessed July 6, 2015. *www.biblestudytools.com/dictionaries/bakers-evangelical-dictionary/levite.html*

18. HENRY. "1 Samuel, chapter 1" *www.biblegateway.com*

19. ACTS 9:17–19

20. 1 PETER 5:7 NIV

21. HENRY. "1 Samuel, chapter 1" *www.biblegateway.com*

22. STRONG, JAMES. "Maidservant." *Strong's Hebrew Concordance.* Accessed November 7, 2015. *www.biblehub. com/hebrew/519.htm*

23. EPHESIANS 4:2 NIV

24. CHERRY, KENDRA. "20 Ways to Improve Your Memory." Accessed May 24, 2015. *www.psychology.about. com/od/memory/tp/20-Ways-to-Improve-Your-Memory.htm*

25. DEFFINBAUGH, BOB. "Israel Gets a King." Accessed November 15, 2015. *www.bible.org/seriespage/17-israel-gets-king-1-samuel-11-1623*

26. HENRY. "1 Samuel, Chapter 2" *www.biblegateway.com*

27. HENRY. "1 Samuel, Chapter 2" *www.biblegateway.com*

28. 2 KINGS 4:8–37 NLT

29. SWOPE, RENEE. *A Confident Heart Devotional*, pg. 113, 2013 ebook edition 2013, Revell, division of Baker Group, Grand Rapids, MI

30. Boncompagni-Hoover, Tatiana. "Yard-Sticking: Do You Do It?" Accessed December 1, 2015. *www.boncompagni.blogspot.com/2012/11/yard-sticking-do-you-do-it.html* (gives original credit for the term to Jennifer Tanner, Rutgers University)

31. Unofficial survey conducted of 100 7th and 8th grade girls using Survey Monkey.

32. Lovatt, Helen. "Roman Noses." Accessed October 26, 2014. *www.blogs.nottingham.ac.uk/argonautsandemperors*

JOURNAL

- Relying on God's promise is my first step in conquering comparison.
— Jeremiah 29:11

"Your eyes saw my substance, yet being unformed. And in your book they all were written, the days fashioned for me, when as yet there were none of them." — Psalm 139:16

"There is surely a future hope for you, and your hope will not be cut off." Prov 23:18

Heartfelt Thanks

Phil, you are the living, breathing evidence of God's blessings in my life. I certainly didn't deserve such a perfect husband, but God brought us together by His grace. God uses you every day to show me what true, unconditional love is all about. Thank you for treating me like a queen.

Garrett, thank you for always knowing how to make me smile. Your sense of humor keeps me from getting too serious! You are my constant reminder of what's most important in life, and I love you.

To *my parents*, you've supported every idea, activity, and new adventure without question or doubt. You showed confidence in my potential, and patience when I insisted on learning some things the hard way. Thank you for the unwavering love and encouragement.

To *Erin, Brittyn, and Ryan,* for taking me on the greatest adventure–becoming a Mimi! I love you three with all my heart.

To *my dear friends*, thank you for the laughs and the tears, but especially the laughs! Thank you for helping me see the greatness of God's plan right in front of me. You are each on a unique path as well, and I'm glad God allowed ours to intersect.

And finally, to *my Savior*. Thank you for finding this confused young girl when I seemed to be wandering down every winding road that came along, and setting me on a straight path–the one you chose just for me. I'm amazed daily at all my life is now because of You. All praise and honor for this book belongs to You.

ABOUT THE AUTHOR

Kristine Brown weaves words together in a way that draws readers into the adventures and lessons she shares. Her conversational tone and in-depth Scripture studies leave a lasting impact on her audience. Kristine is a writer, dramatist, life-long educator and mentor. In the same way her descriptions of Bible stories come to life on the page, Kristine also brings women from Scripture to life through her dramatic interpretations. She loves connecting women and teen girls with the women of the Bible through our shared experiences. Kristine finds her greatest joy in being a wife, mom, and Mimi. She lives in Texas with her favorite people ever and two loud but adorable dogs. To read more from Kristine, visit *www.morethanyourself.com*.

In 2014 Kristine and her two friends, Teri and Melissa, launched a non-profit ministry, More Than Yourself, Inc. This ministry provides college scholarships to junior high girls each year through an online essay contest. Information about the scholarship program can be found at *www. morethanyourself.com/scholarships*.

A portion of the proceeds from the sale of each book will directly benefit the More Than Yourself, Inc. scholarship program.

61422484R00108

Made in the USA
Lexington, KY
14 March 2017